Martin Lipka ● Chapels and More: Kokkari's Cultural Heritage

Kokkari is renowned for its natural heritage – the sea, the beaches, the hills and the woodlands (as far as they have survived the devastating bush fires). But there is also a rich cultural heritage which is sometimes over-looked, but no less valuable.

A cautionary note must be inserted beforehand: The underlying definition of "cultural heritage" is very comprehensive. All sorts of human activities that have changed the pristine natural conditions may come into consideration.

The most conspicuous witnesses of the religious heritage are Kokkari's churches and chapels, 26 alto-gether. And there is a secular heritage as well, less spectacular perhaps, but closely interwoven with the village's past and present. It is dealt with after the chapel circuit.

In some cases the explanations must take recourse to the local history. Hence a glimpse at Kokkari's past, which is in itself part of the cultural heritage after all, will be offered in the first place.

The author was born in 1945.
He is a retired teacher of English and History,
and lives in Westphalia, a region of Germany.

He is also the author of the
"Kokkari Walks" hiking map.

Free download:
www.lipka-online.de > Kokkari (Samos)

Chapels and More :

Kokkari's Cultural Heritage

Martin Lipka

Third, improved edition

Bibliografische Information der Deutschen Nationalbibliothek:

Die Deutsche Nationalbibliothek verzeichnet diese Publikation in der Deutschen Nationalbibliografie.

Detaillierte bibliografische Daten sind im Internet abrufbar über http://dnb.d-nb.de

Eine deutsche Ausgabe ist erhältlich:

„Kapellen und mehr:
Kokkaris kulturelles Erbe"

ISBN-13: 9783738625929

Herstellung und Verlag:
BoD - Books on Demand, Norderstedt

© 2016 by Martin Lipka

ISBN-13: 9783738618211

Contents

Dedicated to

Μάνος † και Ελευθερία Αμυρσώνης

Foreword

After thoroughly enjoying quite a few vacations on Samos, I started working on this booklet (as well as the "Kokkari Walks" map) with a double purpose in mind: first, to give something back to Kokkari and the Kokkarians; and second, to draw other tourists' attention to unnoticed treasures of the village and its immediate surroundings.

I cannot claim to be a well-established specialist in Greek studies. On the contrary, my Greek language skills must be considered as rather lamentable, a fact that proves particularly limiting when researching the local history. Nevertheless I hope that the booklet will earn itself a favourable acceptance.

The absence of coloured illustrations is intentional: The basic concept of the project is to encourage the readers to venture an on-site inspection and to see for themselves – all sights are within a perimeter of 3 miles, or at most one and a half hour's walk, from the village.

A German edition of the booklet is available. The chance to create a Greek version depends on the prospect whether a translator can be found who will apply herself or himself to the task.

If, some day in the future, a pictorial counterpart of the booklet can be published remains to be seen.

In the meantime, I apologize for any errors or mistakes I may have committed here. Whoever can contribute a correction or an addition is kindly invited to contact

<u>sitemail ⌊ατ⌋ lipmax.de</u>

March 2016
Martin Lipka

A Look at Kokkari's Historical Background

 When seen from Outer Space, the area of Kokkari does not resemble the little red onion to which the village's name is referred (▷ p. 130). It rather looks like a scallop, such as the shell of St. James: From the centre at the well-sheltered bay the valleys radiate into the hills, each of them with an age-old neighbourhood of its own – notably *Mána*, *Aiogdítes* (or *Agiodítes*, ▷ p. 99), *Giánnides*, *Karás*, *Lagáda*, *Lemós*, and *Vígles*. Together they form a watershed which is drained by two brooks, *Mána* in the west and *Tholoréma* in the east, and some unnamed and seasonally dry rivulets from the valleys in between. At the foot of the hills their waters have produced four small plains and the *Kámbos*, the former wetland that extends towards the Long Beach, nowadays drained to facilitate the expansion of the village. The rugged coastline further in the east and west occasionally opens for a cove with a secluded beach.

The local history of these 20 or so square kilometres is embedded in the regional history of Samos as an Aegean island, and in the history of Greece in general. It must not be forgotten that Kokkari never boasted

11

much prominence among the island's villages, at least not before the surge of tourism in the last few decades.

This is why Kokkari's past has been less profoundly researched than that of some other corners of Samos; nevertheless there are a few historical sources to rely on, plus the information gained from present-day Kokkarians.

Antiquity and Middle Ages

The Kokkari area was inhabited in the Bronze Age (about 2000 BC), if not earlier, and certainly during Greek and Roman antiquity. This is attested by the Asklepeios sanctuary at the *Mána* spring (about 500 BC; ▷ p. 38) and also by other archaeological evidence. However, there have been no systematic excavations like those at the south coast.

Whether there was a settlement in the location of today's village centre is not known. Probably those early farming communities preferred the security behind the foothills to a settlement at the coastline, as the Aegean Sea was traditionally plagued with the raids of pirates. On the other hand the bay may have been the operating base of a few fishermen.

The Islamic expansion in the middle of the 7th century AD made the Mediterranean Sea the frontier between Christian and Muslim countries. More than ever pirates and marauders from both sides ravaged the shores. Refuge forts, such as *Kástro Louloudás* (▷ p. 134), came into use again to increase the security of the scattered settlements.

As the Byzantine Empire reorganized its defences, one naval *théma* (military and administrative district) was named after Samos. Comprising the major islands in the Eastern Aegean and the adjacent mainland coast, it provided ships and crews for the Byzantine fleet. In 911, this contribution amounted to 22 warships, 3,980 oarsmen and 600 marine soldiers.

Byzantine Eagle

After the downfall of the Seldjuk sultanates around 1300, several Muslim principalities emerged in Western Anatolia, thus bringing Islam to the shores of the Aegean Sea, including the *Mykáli* peninsula, face to face with Samos! The Eastern Aegean was more than ever a dangerous region to live in, although the sea was still dominated by the Christian powers of Byzantium, Venice and Genoa in turn.

It was the conquest of Constantinople by the Ottoman Empire in 1453 that created a profoundly new situation.

Samos had been ruled by the Giustiniani, a Genoese trading house, for several decades. In the 1470s the Giustiniani withdrew to their main base in *Chíos*, urging the native Samians to seek refuge there as well. For the next 90 years the island remained a no man's land although officially claimed by Stamboul since 1502. Those few inhabitants who had stayed would have been without any protection in the coastal area, so they kept to their hideaways in the hills and mountains. It is no wonder that Samos was considered uninhabited in those decades.

Ottoman Rule

About the middle of the 16th century a systematic resettlement, now under Turkish rule, was initiated by an Ottoman naval officer, *Uluj Ali*. He was an Italian pirate from Calabria who had converted to Islam.

He may have cast an eye on Samos when returning from a naval raid in the Western Mediterranean. Some sources say that he was impressed by the beauty and fertility of the island. But he may have been even more interested in its potential as a naval station off the west coast of Asia Minor, with a strategic location on the route from the Bosporus to the Levant and to Egypt. Perhaps he was also attracted by Samos's shipbuilding potential. The wood of the Samian black pines is still today considered a choice material in shipbuilding, as witnessed by the boat workshops in *Drakéi*.

Tughra ("signature")
of Suleiman the
Magnificent

At any rate, as early as 1550 Sultan Suleiman the Magnificent had awarded him the administration of Samos for outstanding success in naval battles. In other words, *Uluj Ali* was mandated to redevelop the potential of the island. –

The project gathered momentum from 1562 onwards. The organisation of the resettlement was entrusted to the admiral's former helmsman, a Greek by the name of *Nikólaos Sarakínis*, who built his stronghold not far from the south coast – the *Sarikínis* Tower between *Iréo* and *Mýli*. The choice of this location suggests, by the way, that at the time the focus was on southern Samos, whereas the rugged north coast, apart from *Vathí* and *Karlóvassi*, seemed uninviting. –

At this point a digression to the monastery *Panagía i Vrondianí* (short: *Moní Vrondá*) is appropriate, because its foundation in 1566 by the monks *Iákovos* and *Makários* must doubtlessly be seen in the context of the resettlement.

A local tradition claims that when the construction of the convent was started the area which today is *Vourliótes* was deserted. So the monks were dependent on the help of the backwoodsmen from the adjacent Kokkari neighbourhoods (probably *Giánnides* and *Aiogdítes*; for the latter ▷ p. 99). This implies that these settlements already existed in the 1560s; and even though there are no historical records, they may have continued from the Middle Ages. Later, as long as these neighbourhoods had no church or chapel of their own, *Moní Vrondá* obviously served as a substitute. Today's footpath upwards could be the witness of a *monopáti* that churchgoers have trodden for centuries.

It was only in the late 18th century that the chapel of *Profítis Ilías* in *Aiogdítes* (▷ p. 97) nurtured a parochial identity in the adjacent Kokkari neighbourhoods; whether a resident *pápas* was already installed is doubtful.

In the course of time *Moní Vrondá* had also acquired land in the Kokkari area. In later centuries, the parish churches – first *Panaítsa* and then St. Nicholas – were apparently built on the monastery's estate, as well as at least two chapels, *Ioánnis Pródromos* and *Pandeleímonas*.

Back to Captain *Uluj Ali*: In 1572/73 he had become the admiral of the Ottoman Navy under the title of *Kiliç Ali Pasha*. He asked the Sultan to assign him the island as a personal grant, thus putting his resettlement project under supreme protection and at the same time safeguarding a considerable amount of autonomy for it.

 The settlers were allocated land for cultivation and were individually exempted from taxes for seven years. Samos as a whole was exempted from the *dekati* (tithe) against an annual lump payment of 45,000 piasters. The sultan's grant included the warranty that the only Muslim to be allowed on the island would be the commander. A curious clause stipulated that this official should be restricted to a certain area of the island, and whenever he departed from Samos he should leave his shoes there, to make sure that he did not take away a single grain of dust.

The immigrants came from the Greek and Anatolian mainland as well as from other Aegean islands, including descendants of those Samians who had fled to *Chíos* a hundred years earlier. They were attracted by the generous privileges that prevailed; a particularly far-reaching concession was the clause that no Muslims would be allowed to settle. The religious homogeneity made it easy for the Greek-Orthodox Church to uphold the Christian creed, which indirectly supported the cultural and social coherence among the growing Samian population.

A number of the new Samians had come from *Mytilíni* on the island of *Lésvos* in the north. They landed at the site which is now the village proper of Kokkari. For safety considerations they did not settle here, but moved south to a place beyond the hills, where they founded the village called *Mytilinií* ("the Mytilinians").

16

However, they upheld a small outpost at the north coast as a harbour.

So, in the year 1601 (or 1610?), a place or a person called *Kokar* (▷ p. 130) was mentioned in an Ottoman source for the first time. In 1637 no less than eight taxable persons were registered in the settlement; so there may have been as many families, and a total of 30 to 40 inhabitants. It stands to reason that these figures refer only to the coastal outpost, omitting the population of the rural neighbourhoods.

In the course of time the connection to *Lésvos* lost its importance for the *Mytilinií* villagers, and *Kokar* alias *Kokkári* was temporarily abandoned. Nevertheless the area continued to be a part of the *Mytilinií* territory until the middle of the 19th century. –

In the testament of *Kiliç Ali Pasha*, who had died in 1587, the island was bequeathed as a *vakif* (religious estate) to a mosque in Stamboul that he had founded. This meant a stronger Ottoman influence and a gradual erosion of the privileges, which in turn generated resentment among the local population.

Despite such flaws in the semi-autonomous status of the island the flow of immigrants to Samos continued, and some sort of political structure emerged. In the middle of the 18th century it worked as follows: The *voevod* (a dignitary of the Ottoman Empire) was at the head of the administration, assisted by the *kadi* (judge), by the local bishop, and by four notables, one from each of the four districts: *Vathí, Chóra, Karlóvassi, Maratho-kámbos*. These notables were elected for a year by the representatives of the villages – in other words, by the wealthy landowning families. The most important task of the administration was to make sure that the tax was collected as decreed in 1572.

In the second half of the 18th century Samos experienced an economic upturn, not least because of its trade connections throughout the Mediterranean, which of course favoured the development of coastal settlements.

Kokkari's ruins were also settled again. The newcomers, attracted by the well-sheltered bay, either came down from their inland homesteads, or arrived by boat from other islands. The first *Panagía* church (▷ p. 46) was founded. Together with the modest *platía* 25 metres away, the site of the little church marked the centre of the village as it gradually developed and expanded onto the hill on one side, and across the brook that flows into the bay on the other. –

During the Fifth Russo-Turkish War (1771-1774) Samos was occupied by the Russian Baltic Fleet under Admiral Alexei Orlov. For Russia the peace treaty opened the way to the northern shores of the Black Sea, and to the annexation of the Crimea some years later. The Tsar's role as the protector of the Orthodox Christians living in the Ottoman Empire was now officially acknowledged by the Sultan. But the hopes that Samos might be liberated from Turkish rule had come to nothing. –

In the following decades Samian intellectuals and businessmen banded together in a progressive movement which was inspired by Western ideas, especially by the French Revolution. They called themselves the *Karma-nióli* – "La Carmagnole" was a popular song of revolutionary France. Under the leadership of *Likoúrgos Logothétis*, they temporarily brought about a liberalisation in the island's fiscal and economic policies (1807-1812), which enhanced the prospects of the littoral settlements.

As far as Kokkari is concerned, the *Panaítsa* village church (▷ p. 49) was built in 1819, replacing the first *Panagía* as the parish church. The new location suggests a shift in the development to the right bank of the village brook.

It is an interesting question whether this conspicuous division reflected different modes of life – perhaps with the fishermen at the foot of the village hill, next to the well-sheltered *Limáni*, the merchants in the flat areas, and the agricultural families further back?

A worn-out street sign opposite the northeast gate to the forecourt of the *Panaítsa* reads: *ΟΔΟΣ ΨΑΡΩΝ*. Not "Fish Street", as one might think, but, as community president *George Pérris* points out, the residential area of people who many generations ago immigrated from *Psará*, a village at the southern tip of the neighbouring island of *Chios*.

This lane, narrow as it may seem, was also part of the old Kokkari thoroughfare. Approaching from the southeast (i.e. from *Vathí*), the track first skirted the southwest slope of *Tepé* hill and then dropped into the flatlands of the brook. Turning right and then left again, it crossed the brook by today's footbridge. Then it entered the *Platía* from the southeast and continued northwest along the western foot of the hill. 20 metres before it hit the coastline it took a sharp bend to the left and followed the Long Beach.

It should be kept in mind that this track was not laid out as a road or at least a cart track from the start. In the beginning it was by all probability just a mule trail. But it became Kokkari's main axis until the main street was laid out as a tangential road around 1900. This is confirmed by the choice of the site for the village church of 1819, with the school next door (▷ p. 49, ▷ p. 116).

In 1828, when Samos already counted a population of 27,125, the coastal settlement was still a tiny village of just 77 inhabitants, with a majority of 46 males against 31 females. But in the course of the century Kokkari would experience a steady growth.

The Hegemony (Principality) of Samos

In 1821 the Samians took a very active part in the Greek uprising, contributing in *Likoúrgos Logothétis* a leader of national fame, and fighting successfully both on land and on sea. But the expulsion of the island's Turkish garrison was only short-lived.

In the so-called London Protocol of 1832, Great Britain, France and Russia pronounced their final decision that the islands in the Eastern Aegean should be kept by the Ottoman Empire. There was, however, an extra clause stipulating that Samos, in contrast to the other islands, should be granted a special status as the autonomous "Principality of

Samos". The Sublime Porte, i.e. the Ottoman government, implemented the clause as follows:

The Hegemon or Prince, appointed by the Sultan, had to be a Greek-speaking Orthodox Christian. A flat-rate tax of 400,000 piasters was to be paid annually to the Sublime Porte. Muslims were still forbidden to settle on the island – an aspect which accounted for the attraction of Samos in the eyes of prospective Greek immigrants. In some way this was an echo of the privileges that had been granted to *Kiliç Ali Pasha* in 1572.

So, although the island was not included in the Greek fatherland, it should still have been in a favoured position to pursue its economic advantages, not only in agriculture (wine, olive oil, tobacco, leather), but also in trade, especially as the autonomy meant that the Samian harbours enjoyed some characteristics of a free port. However, in the following decades Samos saw much inner unrest. The war exertions of the island had resulted in an economic crisis, with widespread poverty and gang delinquency.

On top of this, the rift in the politically active sector of the population widened between those who saw their advantage in subservient collaboration with the first hegemon, *Stéphanos Vogorídis*, and those whose hopes for union with Greece had been utterly frustrated. For *Vogorídis* this was a welcome constellation to establish a harsh authoritarian rule, and to squeeze additional money from the inhabitants.

It was only in 1849 that a local revolution led to his overthrow. Under the new hegemon, *Aléxandros Kallimáchis*, a constitutional system was introduced in 1850, providing for the separation of the legislative, executive and judicial powers.

What seems a moderately progressive system by the standards of the middle 19th century must be seen in the context of the island's social fabric. The semi-feudal dominance of wealthy landowners and successful wholesale merchants remained undisputed; especially the tenants and day labourers had no choice but to abide by their patrons' political leanings. In the background the Ottoman guard, which had been stationed permanently on Samos from 1850 onwards, would have been at hand in the case of another uprising.

Kallimáchis, the new hegemon, also promoted the development of the island by initiating the establishment of schools, law courts, and a printing house. The question whether Kokkari's school was founded in those years could not be positively ascertained.

All in all there is no doubt that Kokkari participated in the island's gradual progress. An important signal was, around 1860, the separation from *Mytilinií* and the establishment as a self-contained community – a *dímos* ("town" or "municipality") according to the terminology of the hegemony. This meant that Kokkari was entitled to elect its own representative to the Samian Parliament.

Yet there existed one last reminder of the connection to *Mytilinií*: As late as in the 1899 Samos Yearbook, Kokkari was included in the *Mytilinií* statistics of the *Chóra* district. The curious consequence was that the new community interrupted the territory of the *Vathí* district along the north coast, making the villages further west, around the Nightingale Valley, an exclave.

At this point a side glance at the role of Kokkari's outlying neighbourhoods seems necessary. Before the communal reform, and sometimes even after, their affiliation to the village of Kokkari proper was somewhat haphazard. This means that at least the population figures before the 1860s may refer to the coastal settlement only.

A good case in point is *Aiogdítes* (see also p. 99). The Samos Yearbook of 1875 still describes it as a *Vourliótes* hamlet. Unfortunately the population statistics below the municipality level are piecemeal, so that an inconsistency might have passed unnoticed. –

Perhaps the new municipality of Kokkari was among the initiators of a donation to Hegemon *Miltíadis Aristárchis* in the early 1860s. The Samian Parliament honoured the hegemon by granting him a large patch of fertile land in Kokkari's *Kámbos*. However, this friendly gesture did not prevent the islanders from overthrowing him in a revolt some years later.

The land in question, about 18,000 square metres, equalling two football pitches, has been remembered ever since by the name of *Aristárchis*. After passing through different hands, it was eventually sold by the *Elissavítis* family to the municipality. Today the by-pass

road cuts right through. The communal sports ground and the new medical outpost mark the southern half of the original plot.

The local football club proudly carries the name *Aristárchos* in the weatherworn plate at the wall of its meeting shack in the main street, about 100 metres east of the parish church. But beware! The scraggy-haired patron saint of the emblem does not represent Hegemon *Aristárchis*, but the almost homonymous great astronomer Aristarchos of Samos (3rd century BC)! And Kokkari's football heroes nowadays play on a pitch in Samos town. –

In the second half of the 19th century the Kokkarians lived mainly on farming and fishing. The local agricultural sector must have been quite varied, with the fertile flatlands and sun-drenched hill slopes around. Today's olive groves are a reminder of a crop that earned many a generation a modest living.

In the 1864 census Kokkari was still included in the 3,404 inhabitants categorized under *Mytilinii* (Samos total: 33,998). But in the light of the 1875 figures there can be no doubt that the village had caught up with the general development of the hegemony. The population statistics from 1875 to 1899 give individual figures for Kokkari, marking a growth by 67 % within a quarter of a century (from 654 to 1,092; Samos as a whole: from 34,141 to 52,775, i.e. by 54 %).

The Hegemony's Coat of arms: lion's head, bull and peacock (postal stamp, 1878)

It may be mentioned in passing that in 1876 the well near the *Platía* (▷ p. 118) marked the advent of public utilities.

From a Western or Central European point of view the Principality of Samos

24

seemed a somewhat exotic spot. But its political opinion leaders took pride in the island's special status. Samos not only established its own postal service, but even entertained consular relations with the major European powers.

In 1898 Paul Lindau, a German intellectual, stopped on Samos for a few days. In his travelogue he commented somewhat condescendingly on the "operetta state" of the hegemony and on the personality of the Hegemon himself. He claimed that there was only one horse-drawn carriage on the island, which, he added, was no wonder because there were no roads anyway.

And yet it was this same hegemon, *Stéphanos Mousoúros* (1896-1899), under whose government the Samians undertook to build several overland roads linking the main localities, including the connection between *Vathí* and *Karlóvassi* along the north coast. The first road on Samos, between *Vathí* and *Mytilinií*, had already been initiated by the hegemon's uncle, Hegemon *Pávlos Mousoúros*, around 1870. Despite such efforts, though, the land-based traffic network remained inadequate, and deficient maintenance was a permanent source of complaints by the haulers.

At any rate, in the late 1890s Kokkari got its first "modern" road, namely the main street. Its route was designed to follow a straight course, bypassing the village centre. The view up and down this thoroughfare covers almost 500 metres. When the site for the present-day parish church was chosen a few years later (▷ p. 53), the short crosslink connecting the northwest exit of the *Platía* to the main street was taken as a cue: St. Nicholas was given a dominant position on the other side. The decision in favour of such an ambitious building project reflects the steady progress Kokkari had seen during the last decades of the 19th century. –

In 1904 Samos was struck by a strong earthquake; 4 persons died, 540 houses were destroyed. It was not possible to find out to what extent Kokkari was affected. –

Although the second half of the 19th century turned out less chaotic for the island than the decades before, internal antagonisms and enmities as well as the perennial aversion against the Ottoman overlords and their local supporters erupted every once in a while in riots and assassinations.

The 20th Century

During the first decade of the new century, the tension between pro-Greek and pro-autonomy (by implication pro-Ottoman) factions escalated. The most ardent advocate of the union with Greece was *Themistoklís Sofoúlis*, an archaeologist born on Samos who had turned politician.

In May 1908 *Andréas Kopásis*, a hard-line hegemon, called in the regular Turkish military. In the riots that erupted several Samians were killed. And in Kokkari the construction works of the new parish church, begun in 1902, were interrupted for the next 25 years (▷ p. 53).

After the setback of 1908, the political climate remained explosive. When the coalition of Greece, Serbia,

Bulgaria and Montenegro invaded the Ottoman Empire in the First Balkan War (1912), *Sofoúlis* returned from his exile and declared the union of Samos with Greece. Later, as the leader of a centre-left party, he became a politician of national influence until his death in 1949.

In 1913/14, the national census of Greece counted 1,514 Kokkarians. In the course of the 19th century the population balance had turned in favour of the village proper; the neighbourhoods in the safety of the hills noticeably lost their attraction as places to dwell in. –

Inadvertently the integration into the Kingdom of Greece had weakened the island's economic connections to the west coast of Asia Minor. This would become painfully clear in the First Wold War and its aftermath.

The problem was exacerbated when the ill-conceived Greek invasion of western Anatolia collapsed in 1922. The perennial antagonism between Greeks and Turks erupted

Royal Coat of Arms 1863 – 1924: "My power is the love of the people"

in sheer hatred. Samos was one of the first places to witness the flood of refugees from the Asian mainland. Thus the 1928 census recorded 1536 Kokkari residents, the largest figure ever (after only 1385 in 1920). But the refugees tended to proceed to the Greek mainland, and even among native Samians emigration was on the increase, boosted even further in the 1930s by the Great Depression.

So it was a daring decision to start work on St. Nicholas again in 1933. But five years later the edifice, although not yet completed, could actually be used as Kokkari's parish church.

On the other hand the regional economic problems, together with the political instability of Greece, slowed down the further development of the island. The World Economic Crisis had made things even more complicated. The EOSS (Samos Wine Cooperative, founded in 1934) was meant to relieve the problems. Looking back from the 2010s, the mandatory membership is considered a setback by some wine growers.

In 1940 Greece was a dictatorship under *Ioánnis Metaxás*, whose regime was modelled on the patterns of Italian fascism. Even so, when Italy threatened to invade the country, *Metaxás* rejected the ultimatum. This is the origin of Επέτειος του ΟΧΙ ("Anniversary of *Ochi*", a.k.a. "No!"-Day). It is celebrated each year all over Greece, and of course also in Kokkari, on October 28. – This "No!" actually marks the entry of the country into the Second World War, albeit against its will.

The Italian attack was pushed back, but the German Balkan campaign in April 1941 compelled Greece to capitulate. Samos was put under Italian occupation. Some minor fortification works at Kokkari's coastline (▷ p. 137) may go back to the years of the Second World War.

On the island, as elsewhere in Greece, local underground groups waged a partisan war against the occupiers. In retaliation to a resistance raid, Italian troops massacred 27 male inhabitants of *Kastanía*, a small village south of *Karlóvassi*, on August 30, 1943. Among the victims was a boy of just 15.

A change of the tide seemed at hand when in September 1943 Italy capitulated and the Allied forces tried to exploit the situation by pushing into the eastern Aegean Sea. A Greek special force, known as *Ierós Lóchos* ("Sacred Band", after a Theban elite force, 4th c. BC), invaded Samos in the night of October 30/31. It had been formed in Egypt by the British Army from exiled Greek officers. The commandos either parachuted onto the *Vlamaris* plain or arrived by fisher boats. There is a memorial next to the Monastery of *Zoodóchos Pigí* east of Samos Town.

However, the liberation was only short-lived. The Allied offensive had been improvised, and it soon collapsed under the German counterattack; Samos was given up in the night of November 19/20. Two days later the German storm troops were landed (▷ p. 142, postscript). Afterwards the occupation was upheld by Wehrmacht units consisting mainly of soldiers from the "Ostmark", i.e. Austrians.

Ten months later, in September 1944, the hasty German retreat from the Greek mainland and most of the islands offered a better chance. According to German sources no occupation troops were left on Samos. Still there may have remained a few stragglers who surrendered either to the local Resistance or to the Sacred Band, who landed again on October 4.

The German and Italian occupants had exploited Greece as best they could, leaving behind an impoverished nation. Adequate indemnities for the losses of human life or for the damages have never been paid.

The post-war period aggravated Greece's condition even further. From 1946 to 1949 a civil war tore the nation apart. The left-wing *DSE* (Democratic Army of Greece) fought against the army of the right-wing government. The *DSE* – the continuation of a resistance militia which had led the guerilla war against the German occupation – was backed by the communist governments of Yugoslavia, Albania und Bulgaria. The right-wing National Government had the support of Great Britain and the USA. For the prime minister, Samos-born *Themistoklís Sofoúlis* (▷ p. 26), his coopera-tion with right-wing extremists and reactionaries be-came an evil blemish on his historical record. It was shortly after his death in 1949 that the conflict was eventually decided in favour of the Nationalists and Royalists, because Yugoslavia had withdrawn its support for the *DSE*.

Samos, with its long history of fraternal strife, had a *DSE* battalion, too, and sometimes the political rift went right through the families. There are occasional hints that also men from Kokkari were interned in *Makró-nisos*, off the east coast of Attica. It may well be that the wounds of those years have left scars in the old gene-ration. At any rate it is not easy to gather information in order to understand what such memories meant and still mean locally. A similar reservation applies to the years of the right-wing Military Junta (▷ p. 31). –

The prosecution of leftist activists and the unpropitious economic prospects of the 1950s induced more and more Samians to emigrate to the Greek mainland, to European countries, and worldwide. But most of the expatriates stayed in close contact with their home island, and quite a few returned to spend their old age here.

In the 1960s the shadows of the past were to some extent softened by the island's gradual economic progress. Electrification was a crucial factor. For decades the only light source at home had been the petroleum lamp. Now the island's *DEH* power plant was installed on the coast at the estuary of the *Tholoréma* brook, one kilometre east of Kokkari. The adjacent *SILK* oil tanks furnish the fuel. There is no pier up to this day, so the oil tankers just drop anchor to be unloaded. When the waves go high, the tanker may have to wait in the open roadstead off the Long Beach, which is always a spectacular sight at night. –

From 1967 to 1974, the right-wing Military Junta (a.k.a. the Regime of the Colonels) reopened bitter old rifts in the nation's political landscape. Economically the country continued its arduous upward path.

Greek Republic Coat of Arms, 1975

In 1974/75 Greece left dictatorship and monarchy behind. This paved the way for the accession to the European Community, the predecessor of the European Union, in 1981 – an important milestone in the country's recent history, whether for good or for bad remains to be seen.

The civilian airport near *Pythagório* had been opened in 1963. Its full significance became tangible when the non-stop charter flights began in 1976. They enabled the present-day tourism, which brought new and promising economic options with it, but also changed the visual appearance and the social fabric of the village. Traditional elements supporting social coherence were weakened, while competitive attitudes came to the fore. Investment in real estate promised high returns for those who could fork out the money.

Commercially Kokkari benefited visibly from the new economic sector, as a tourist magnet second only to *Pythagório*. The Long Beach, originally a bare stretch of pebbles and sand, was developed into a more or less coherent row of buildings catering for sunbathers, extending almost as far as the Beach Mill ruin.

Such changes have made agriculture an economic sideline. Even the wealthy landowners of yore have lost much of their influence. Several of these families are extinct because marriage partners of an equal social status could not be found. The smallholders or lease-holders work their fields in the evening or on Saturday, or leave the cultivation entirely to the old generation. And everywhere the traditional goat pen behind the house has been turned into living quarters.

The men from the mountain villages now often take up jobs at the coast or in town, so that up there the day-time population seems to consist of children and old age pensioners. Women may have more opportunities than in the past, but they must also bear more responsibility, and in terms of gender roles Greek families may still be quite conservative. –

To develop the tourist potential of Kokkari's centre around the bay, the breakwater was built in the early 1990s, followed by an upgrade of the promenade along the water front. This benefited the restaurants and bars all round the bay, such as Stathis Restaurant, founded in 1976, or Cavos Cafe Bar, established in 1986.

At about the same time the hotel cluster emerged on the western hills. The largest compound by far, Arion, was started in 1992 by an entrepreneur from *Vourliótes*. More hotels and guesthouses were built on the road to Karlóvassi, typically by local owners rather than external speculators. In retrospect the resolution to keep the village and the littoral free from large hotel blocks deserves great respect.

The last 15 Years

It cannot be denied that the requisites of tourism have changed Kokkari's face, albeit without sacrificing too much of its natural heritage. So much the worse was the devastating bush fire in 2000, when large areas of forest and scrubland, including many of the Kokkari hills, were laid waste. And the danger has not been eliminated, as the 2010 fire shows. –

In 2002 Greece was among the twelve countries that introduced Euro coins and banknotes instead of their previous currencies. At the time parting with the *drachmí* seemed an easy thing to do, but a decade later the problems were bitterly felt when the financial crisis with its economic and social repercussions hit the nation.

One of the counter measures was the *Kallikrátis* Reform of 2011, aiming at the reduction of cost and bureaucracy in regional and local administration. In consequence of the reform, Kokkari is now part of the municipality of Samos (*Dímos Sámou*). Within this frame it is granted a certain amount of autonomy as a *topikí kinótita*.

According to the census of 2011, this "local community" counted 1,060 residents (after only 849 in 1971). The figure is probably doubled during the summer months by seasonal employees in the tourist business. The overall number of tourist beds has been estimated at close to 3,000.

Kokkari seems to be particularly popular with Scandinavians, Dutch, and Germans. How much it now depends on tourism has become clear during the present crisis of Greece. When foreign bookings decrease and regular guests from Athens can no longer afford a vacation, the consequences are immediately felt. The recovery of 2014 was a hopeful sign, but the dramatic crisis a year later has put any certainties in jeopardy.

The result of the referendum on July 5, 2015, can be better understood in the light of the year 1940 (▷ p. 28). But this repetition of the resolute and self-assured "*Oxi!*", "No!", has solved none of of the problems – neither in the interior, where the state, with scant revenues but caught in multiple expenses, faces a daunting reform backlog; nor in the exterior, where the European partners had and still have the ability to help, but demand drastic preconditions.

And in the background there is the predicament of many a Greek citizen who is impassioned by his national pride, but mistrusts his own government outright and is inclined to excuse patronage, corruption and tax evasion as inevitable practices.

Nevertheless it is to be hoped that the friendly people of Kokkari und their pleasant village will retain the affection and respect of their holiday guests.

February 2016

The arrival of tens of thousands of refugees from the Asian mainland since the summer of 2015 has put Samos under enormous strain, even if the island is only a stepping stone on the way to countries further north. And while the Greeks were still berated for their financial shortcomings, whether tangible or alleged, they tried hard to cope with the new challenge. The question stands to reason if its European partners shouldn't give Greece better support.

Orthodox Christianity in Practice

In their traditional self-image the Orthodox Churches consider themselves the only legitimate branch of Christianity and look down on other branches as misguided, if not schismatic or downright heretical. The Roman Catholic Church's position is more or less reciprocal, whereas the Protestant mainstream co-operates with the Orthodoxy in the World Council of Churches.

At any rate the dogmatic differences are much smaller than some zealots would think. This is because they all share the Nicean Creed (▷ p. 68), plus the decisions of several subsequent Ecumenical Councils. But at the level of popular prejudice the damnation as αιρετικός (heretic) can still be encountered.

The traumatic antagonism between East and West, the Great Schism, goes back to 1054. The supremacy of the Pope was only one of several apples of discord, albeit the most perspicuous. This break-up, brought about back then by hotheads on both sides, is still a frequent cause of irritation, despite the conciliatory visit of Pope Francis to the Ecumenical Patriarch Bartholomew I of Constantinople in 2014.

The Ecumenical Patriarch is regarded as the symbolic head and spiritual leader of Eastern Orthodox Christianity as a whole. In all other respects, however, the Church of Greece is an autocephalous, i.e. autonomous, member of the Orthodox κοινωνία ("Communion"), acknowledging no other head than its Holy Synod under the presidency of the Archbishop of Athens.

Ecumenical Patriarch's coat of arms

Even so, for historical reasons the Eastern Aegean islands, including Samos, are still linked to Constantinople: Every new bishop has to be confirmed by the Patriarch and can appeal to him; for all practical purposes, however, the Eastern Aegean dioceses are administered by the Church of Greece "in stewardship".

Chapels

The majority of Kokkari's chapels were built in the 20th century, or possibly in the 19th; only very few are more than two hundred years old. The chapels offer no spectacular highlights, but rather constitute a cross section of all levels of conservation: Some of them are in excellent condition, others are semi-derelict. They were erected by local people, often in consequence of a vow, and may still be looked after by the descendants.

Occasionally a chapel was positioned near the site of a pre-Christian place of worship or even on its ruins.

Take for example the chapel of St. Panteleimon, the "Healer": It is less than 100 yards away from the *Mána* Spring compound, which had been dedicated in Antiquity to Asklepeios, the god of healing in Greek mythology. The stumps of two or three columns of the sanctuary can still be seen under the huge plane trees, while another one lies on the sea floor off the *Mána* estuary. Thanks to the chapel that ancient tradition has found a new meaning as an expression of the Greek people's piety. –

Whenever you approach a church or chapel, try to appreciate the special atmosphere: the embedding in the landscape and in the immediate surrounding, the simplicity or the elaboration of the building. Is the masonry raw quarry stone or white-and-blue plaster? Is there a forecourt or a porch? Is there a cupola on top? And where is the bell? If you are tempted to ring the bell, remember that it may be understood by the local people as a signal with a meaning that you are not aware of.

As far as the outlying chapels are concerned, almost all of them are accessible to the general public. However, you may have to try your hand at some makeshift fastening contraption at the door.

Once inside, enjoy the subdued light, the silence, and the cool temperature. But even if you have entered only for curiosity's sake, remember to respect the religious character of the edifice and behave appropriately.

In general a vaulted roof construction is characteristic of older buildings, while a wooden ceiling, especially when supported by visible rafters, is most probably of a more recent origin.

Somewhere, usually not far from the entrance, there will be an opportunity to take a candle and light it – in a bed of sand, for security reasons. If you decide to emulate this custom, don't forget to drop a coin in the offertory box, usually not more than a wooden chest with an inconspicuous slot on top.

When you leave the chapel, mind the lintel, because it may be quite low; and then remember to close the door and to fix the fastener where necessary.

The Significance of Icons

In every Orthodox church or chapel the so-called iconostasis immediately catches the visitor's eye. It separates the *ágio víma* (sanctuary) with the altar from the congregation in the *klítos* (nave).

The sanctuary is reserved for the priest and the sexton, and a considerate visitor should not enter. Often, however, it is possible to peer inside and see the altar and the apse behind it with the eastern window. This window, tiny though it may be, is a symbolic inlet of the sunrise into the chapel, reminding day by day of the resurrection of Jesus Christ.

The iconostasis is dominated by the Holy Door in the middle, with an icon of Christ on the right and another of the Madonna on the left, as seen from the nave. The patron saint's icon is usually found at the other side of Christ, unless the chapel is dedicated to Holy Mary herself.

Apart from the iconostasis, various other icons may be distributed around the walls. Often they are just simple prints on paper; but Orthodox Christians are convinced that every icon is hallowed after it has been blessed by a priest. It is by no means the icon itself that becomes the object of devotion, but the holy person who is represented, and whose name is inscribed. This inscription is an indispensable feature of an icon, although it is not always easy to decipher, because it is written in a special calligraphy including traditional abbreviations.

Some major icons are accompanied by a number of so-called *tamáta*, small silvery plaques. Such a *táma* is a votive gift by which somebody appeals to the saint for intercession or gives the saint thanks for successful assistance. Very often the embossed image reveals the nature of the supplicant's concern.

When parts of the painting are covered with a silvery metal sheet, the icon deserves special attention: Maybe it is believed to have been the instrument of a miracle, and the silver coating may express the gratitude of the miracle's beneficiary. By the way, the sheet has a very practical function as well: It makes it possible for the many faithful to kiss the icon without doing any damage to the painting itself. Such a silvery cover is of course more appropriate than the simple glass pane of our days.

Summing up, for the faithful an icon is not a work of art, whether worthless or valuable, but a sacred object enabling the devout person to come closer to God. So it should be a matter of course for Westerners to respect the icons as well as the underlying belief.

Giortés – the Traditional Chapel Feasts

In the course of the year many a Kokkari chapel is the scene of a popular feast to celebrate the memory of the patron saint. The Greek word γιορτή comprises three essential aspects of these feasts:

- the religious feast of the saint in question,
- the cheerful meeting of the local residents, often combined with a nightly vigil beginning on the previous day,
- and, last but not least, the traditional festive meal, prepared during the vigil and shared in the morning after the liturgy.

The date of the feast follows the ecclesiastical calendar of the Greek-Orthodox Church, which begins on September 1. About half of those events take place in the hot summer months when the vigil can hope for comfortable early morning temperatures.

The following list is without guarantee:

September 26   *Agios Ioánnis Theólogos* (▷ p. 88)

October 26   *Agios Dimítrios* (▷ p. 71, ▷ p. 100)

November 21   *Panagía / Isodía Theótokou* (▷ p. 86)

December 6   *Agios Nikólaos* (▷ p. 53)

April 23 or Easter Monday   *Agios Giórgios* (▷ p. 102)

Friday after Easter   *Panagía / Zoodóchos Pigí* (▷ p. 73)

Monday after Pentecost   *Agía Triáda* (▷ p. 67)

July 20   *Profítis Ilías* (▷ p. 93, ▷ p. 97)

July 26   *Agía Paraskeví* (▷ p. 71, ▷ p. 75)

July 27   *Agios Pandeleímonas* (▷ p. 107)

August 6   *Metamórfosis* (▷ p. 69)

August 15   *Panagía / Kímisis* (▷ p. 96)

August 23   *Panagía / "Enniámera" Kímisi* (▷ p. 49)

August 27   *Agios Fanoúrios* (▷ p. 110)

August 29   *Agios Joánnis Pródromos* (▷ p. 82,
              ▷ p. 105)

The feast at the *Pandeleímonas* chapel in the *Mána* valley on July 27 is said to be most prestigious of them all, attracting participants from all over Samos.

The festive meal

According to the young *Exoklísia* authors (▷ p. 141), the custom of the festive meal originates from Asia Minor, and may go back to the agape of early Christian times. The agape was a communal meal to which each participant contributed some food and wine. Another root of the custom may be the offering of *tamáta*, votive gifts.

The visitors of a saint's feast may often have to walk a considerable distance, so they arrive in the evening of the previous day and spend the night at the chapel, either keeping a vigil or lying down for a short sleep. In the morning a liturgical service is held, and then everybody enjoys the *giortí* meal, traditionally consisting of "meat, onions, and wheat". The *Exoklísia* authors describe the typical sequence of events as follows:

The preparation of the meal lies in the hands of some *mastóri*, "master cooks"; the *Exoklísia* mentions a team of four "masters". The procedure starts on the eve of the feast when a fire is lit under a large cauldron. First of all goat meat, about 25 kilograms, is thoroughly stewed, before it is sprinkled with a package of salt and skimmed. After some hours the meat can be boned, and then 25 kilos of onions are added.

In the meantime the master cooks and the bystanders taste some *mezédes* ("appetizers") and douse them with wine, *soúma* or *oúzo*. Later they may take a short sleep.

In the morning between 5 and 6 o'clock it is time to add 25 kilos of wheat, together with 2 kilos of oil and 4 kilos of butter. From now on the stew must be stirred steadily with a wooden oar or ladle so that it does not stick too much, but takes on a creamy consistence. This is an exhausting and time-consuming procedure, so the cooks take it in turns until about 9 o'clock.

After the morning liturgy the *pápas*, the local priest, will bless the meal by sprinkling it with holy water, and then it is dished out to the congregation.

This standard *giortí* meal is modified in the

fasting period and also on the feasts of John the Baptist (August 29) and Transfiguration (August 6), when the meat is replaced by chick peas or octopus. This can easily be explained in the case of the Lenten season; in the case of John the Baptist his death by beheading may account for the vegetarian recipe.

Wayside Shrines

An attentive observer will occasionally notice a wayside shrine, often in the shape of a miniature chapel. This is the plain man's version of a chapel – a printed icon and an oil lamp will do. Thus it does not require much in terms of cost and maintenance, but of course the shrine goes without the benefits of ecclesiastical rituals and the *giortí* (feasts).

The best-known wayside shrine is the exemplar in modern style at the Limp Mill Arch. Another shrine is located opposite Hotel  *Mýlos Beach* at the junction of the narrow ascending road.

The white shrine at the waterfront walk near the *Platía* is a different case: It is a memorial with a special significance (▷ p. 46).

The Chapel Circuit

The parish of Kokkari counts 26 chapels – or, more precisely, two churches, 23 chapels, and one special shrine reminding of the village's first church. The sequence of the following compilation offers an itinerary which starts in the village and then moves clockwise around the outlying areas, so that it covers all 26 locations in the end. The consecutive numbering helps to find the respective location in the map sketches from ▷ p. 143 onwards.

The GPS coordinates are given in the pattern GG°MM.mmm' (grades and minutes, the latter with three decimal places), followed by the altitude in metres.

Churches and Chapels in the Village

1. Panagía (Holy Mary), commemorative shrine

N037°46.773′ E026°53.588′ // 2m // map ▷ p. 143

By-name: *Kímisis tis Theotókou* ("Dormition of the Birth-giver to God", i.e. of the Mother of God).

The peculiar shrine on the harbour promenade, 25 metres north of the *Platía*, is easily over-looked in passing. And yet the white cubes with their blue caps are a reminder of Kokkari's first village church, and according to local sources this part of the village is also called *Panagía*, after the church.

It could not be verified when the *Panagía* was erected, nor when it was dismantled. A tentative estimation would date the origin of the church around 1800. The chapel of *Profítis*

Ilías in the peripheral area of *Aiogdites*, founded in 1786, is generally believed to be older (▷ p. 97).

Of the original church only the altar has been preserved, consisting of four cuboids topped by white doves, and a larger central cuboid which carries a sort of lantern with a superimposed white cross. One of the four lantern windows, namely the one looking towards the hill, can be opened. However, it is advisable to leave it closed, because the inside can be very sooty.

Considering the traditional eastward orientation of church architecture, it would seem that the nave was positioned towards the hill, under the present-day roof structure. So the edifice cannot have been very large. Yet, as local informants assert, it was high enough to boast a gallery in the back, accessible by an outside staircase. This was the *ginekonítis* ("women's section") – which implies that the floor of the nave was reserved for the male half of the congregation.

The church was situated very close to the shore, and at a low elevation. So it must have been under constant threat from the waves, even if the underground may have been solid rock. Sooner or later the construction of a larger church in a safer location was inevitable (▷ p. 49).

Η Παναγία

Panagía, the "All-Holy", is the popular name given in Greek-Orthodox Christianity to the Holy Virgin Mary, Mother of God.

The appellation reflects the belief that among the saints the Virgin Mary ranks above all the others. This is underlined by the fact that four of the Twelve Great Feasts in the course of the Orthodox church year

(September 1 to August 31) are celebrated in honour of the *Theótokos*, the "Birth-giver to God". Each of these feasts may lend its name to a church or chapel dedicated to Holy Mary.

The four Great Feasts in question are:

- the Nativity of the *Theótokos*, on September 8;
- the Presentation (at the Temple) of the *Theótokos* on November 21 (see p. 80);
- the Annunciation to the *Theótokos*, on March 25;
- the Dormition of the *Theótokos* on August 15. The Dormition (*Kímisis*, "falling asleep") actually means her death, or, as both the Greek-Orthodox and the Roman Catholic Church teach, her bodily assumption into heaven (▷ p. 50).

The title "Birth-giver to God" goes back to the Council of Ephesus in 431 AD. It reflects the dogma that Mary gave birth to God the Son (*Theó-tokos*), not only to Jesus Christ in his human nature (*Christó-tokos*). At the same time the word underlines that Mary was a human, in contrast to the notion held by heathen mythologies that a god could only be born by a mother who was a goddess herself.

Additional information

Kokkari's first village church, the *Panagía*, was actually dedicated to the Dormition, the celebration of which is on August 15. It seems that there is no feast of its own nowadays; it is probably included in the feast of the *Panaítsa* church on August 23 (▷ p. 52). –

The male derivative of *Panagía* is *Panagiótis*, a popular first name for men in Greece.

2. Panaítsa (Holy Mary), old village church

N037°46.657′ E026°53.633′ // 5m // map ▷ p. 143

By-name: *Kímisis tis Theotókou* ("Dormition of the Birth-giver to God").

The former parish church is locally known by the name of *Panaítsa*, "little Mary". The reason is not quite clear, considering that it is larger than any of the chapels around Kokkari. Perhaps the affectionate nickname arose when people realized how huge its successor, St. Nicholas, would be (▷ p. 53).

It is situated quietly in the lower eastern part of the village, at the foot of the western slope of *Tepé* hill, at a distance of about 150 yards from the present-day parish church, and surrounded by a small square.

The appearance of the building, with its octagonal cupola above the double barrel vault of the wide nave, together with its fenced forecourt, demonstrates that it is more than just a simple chapel. Having replaced the first *Panagía* (▷ p. 46) in 1819, it served as Kokkari's parish church for more than one century until this function was transferred to *Agios Nikólaos* in 1938 (▷ p. 53).

Unfortunately the chapel is closed to the public most of the time. Still there is a chance of access during the Easter days and of course during the festive days from August 15 to August 25, the *enniámera*, the "nine days" following the feast of the Dormition.

Η Παναγία

The church is dedicated to the *Panagía*, the "All-Holy" (i.e. the Virgin Mary, Mother of God), or more precisely to the *Kímisi tis Theotókou* ("Dormition", i.e. falling asleep, "of the Birth-giver to God"). The feast is known in Western Christianity as the Assumption (August 15).

Although the death of Holy Mary is vaguely alluded to in some books of the New Testament, the details of the legend are derived from several apocryphal texts.

It is believed that when she was lying on her deathbed in Jerusalem (more likely than in Ephesus), eleven of the twelve apostles were miraculously transported to the place, each of them from the part of the world where he was preaching at the time.

When the corpse was carried to a tomb in the Garden of Gethsemane at the foot of the Mount of Olives, the Jewish priest *Antónios* tried to deride the solemn procession and to topple the funeral bier. But an angel appeared and punished him by cutting off his hands. When *Antónios* repented and became a Christian, he got his hands miraculously back (icon ▷ p. 97).

When the twelfth apostle, Thomas, arrived from India on the third day, he begged to see the deceased for the last time. They discovered that the tomb was empty except for her grave wrappings, and concluded that she had been assumed bodily into heaven. Thomas was inconsolable for having been late. But that night, Holy Mary appeared to him in a dream and promised to send him a sign to still his grief, and when he awoke, he found that she had dropped her *zóni* on him. This Greek word may be translated as belt, cincture, girdle, or sash.

In Jerusalem, the Church of the Sepulchre of Holy Mary is believed to mark the place of her tomb.

The *Agía Zóni*, the "Holy Belt" of the legend, is commemorated by the monastery of the same name in the *Vlamarís* plain east of Samos town.

Additional information

The old church is lavishly endowed and kept in perfect order. The iconostasis, made of dark wood and abundantly adorned, creates a mystical atmosphere. The painting of Holy Mary's deathbed is almost completely covered with silver sheet, only the heads of the different persons can be seen. And above as well as below the icon strings with many silvery votive gifts silently speak of the help that people in distress have found by the intercession of the Mother of God. Holy Mary is also depicted in a notable *Zoodóchos Pigí* icon (▷ p. 67). Taking a cue from the dates on some frescoes, the church must have been renovated in the 1990s.

The conspicuous wooden construction of a table under a canopy supported by four columns is the symbolic bier of Holy Mary. It plays a central role in the festivities in honour of the *Panagía*, when it is lavishly adorned with flowers. –

The feast of the Dormition (August 15) is one of the Twelve Great Feasts, each of which is followed by a celebratory eight-day-period called *enniámera*, "nine days", because the starting day is also counted.

This explains why the feast of the old village church is postponed to August 23. It starts on the eve with a night liturgy, including songs in praise of the *Panagía* and a procession in which her symbolic bier and shroud are carried around. After a vigil in the square the new day is welcomed with another liturgy, followed by the traditional *giortí* meal. –

The church and the square are apparently located on a plot that formerly belonged to the estate of *Móni Vrondá*. The part of the square to the right of the church was Kokkari's first graveyard. The date of its abandonment could not be ascertained, but it would seem that the setup of the present-day cemetery (▷ p. 60) was somehow connected to the construction of the parish church St. Nicholas (▷ following chapter).

3. Ágios Nikólaos (St. Nicholas), parish church

N037°46.677′ E026°53.542′ // 4m // map ▷ p. 143

There is a general conviction among the Kokkarians that St. Nicholas is the largest and most impressive church in all of Samos.

The plans had been drawn by architect *Angelos Angelídis*. The cornerstone was laid in 1902, as the inscription says: "The Hegemon of Samos, *Alexandros Mavrogenos*, and the *archieregontos*, *Athanasios Kapoural*is [also known as *Kapoláris*, at the time metropolitan of Samos, i.e. archbishop], laid this cornerstone on 18 September 1902, during the term of mayor *Fótios Fragoúlis Garoufális*." This was a very ambitious project indeed, and more than once in the course of the following decades it overtaxed the financial capacities of the congregation.

For the building a site had been chosen outside the village, on the far side of the main road, which had been laid out a few years earlier. The lot had been acquired from a monastery, probably *Moní Vrondá*.

The first six years of the construction proceeded steadily; the finances were fed by a lottery initiated by the energetic mayor, *Fótios Garoufális*. But in 1908 the mayor's political opponents persuaded Hegemon *Andréas Kopásis* to repeal the permission of the lottery, with the consequence that the works stopped and were not to be resumed for a quarter of a century.

The stoppage by *Kopásis* in 1908 falls into the larger context of the increasing tensions between the pro-Greek and pro-autonomy factions mentioned in the history chapter. In the years to follow, the political climate remained unfavourable to the church project, from the Balkan War in 1912 to the collapse of the Greek military offensive in Anatolia in 1922.

In the 1920s and 1930s the Greek nation suffered from political and economic instability. So it seemed as if the church would forever stay a ruin. But in 1933 *Ioánnis Elissavítis*, a wealthy citizen of Kokkari, took a courageous decision: He vouched for the entire cost of the completion (▷ p. 119).

On September 30 that year, a solemn procession, with *Irinéos*, the Samos metropolitan, at its head, moved from the old parish church to the half-finished new church to consecrate it for the restart of the works.

The authors of the *Exoklísia* report: "From that day on, everything ran like clockwork: the time schedule, the donations, the workforce. Over five years the whole congregation helped, whether small or tall, rich or poor, man or woman. They transported material, climbing up and down the stairs and the scaffolding – a sea of people coming and going. Boats hauled stones from the quarries at Cape *Kótsika*, and sand from the beaches of *Seïtáni*, *Potámi*, and *Karlóvassi*."

In 1938 the congregation eventually took possession of the new parish church, led by *Pápas Geórgios Partsáfas*. The inscription on the foot of the pillar to the right of the Holy Door probably commemorates the contractor: "*Ergon / N. Peraki / 1938.*"

However, some parts of the church were still unfinished. After further interruptions caused by the Second World War, by the Civil War, and by lack of finances, the church was eventually completed in 1962, after a total of 60 years.

It is indeed a magnificent basilica, 34 metres long and 18 metres wide, with two sturdy towers, a transept, and a cupola 24 metres high above the crossing.

The imposing west front with the stairs, the three arches of the majestic porch, and the main gates is framed by the bell tower on the left und the clock tower on the right. Unfortunately the clock has quite a haphazard idea of time. The bells, on their part, compete for acoustical supremacy with the hundreds of swallows nesting below the facade's upper ledge.

Άγιος Νικόλαος, Ο Θαυματουργός

St. Nicholas (270-343) was the archbishop of Myra on the south coast of Asia Minor (now Demre, Turkey). His name *Nikólaos*, "victory of the people", is often followed by the epithet *Thavmaturgós*, "wonder-worker".

The most popular report on St. Nicholas tells how he helped three young girls. Their father was so poor that he could not afford their dowries, which meant that the daughters would remain unmarried and reduced to a life of squalor, if not prostitution. The saint, who led a very modest life although he had inherited some money, learned about their plight. When the eldest girl came of age, he tiptoed to the house at night and threw a purse with gold coins through the window. He repeated his good turn when the other two girls came of age.

The third time, however, the father had stayed awake to find out who was their mysterious benefactor. But St. Nicholas, who may have had a foreboding, dropped the purse through the chimney this time, and it fell into a stocking that the girl had washed and hung there to dry.

On a pilgrimage to Jerusalem St. Nicholas saved the ship from sinking in a storm by his prayers.

When he had become the bishop of Myra, the town was struck by a severe famine. One day a ship from Egypt with wheat for Rome or Byzantium anchored in the harbour. St. Nicholas begged for part of the cargo to feed his starving fellow citizens. The sailors feared that they would run into trouble at their destination because they had contracted to deliver a certain weight of grain to the emperor. But the saint assured them that they would suffer no loss, and in the end they consented. When the ship arrived in the capital, they found to their surprise that the weight of the load had not changed, although the wheat they had left at Myra had been enough for two years.

In all likelihood St. Nicholas participated in the First Council of Nicaea in 325, and he is believed to have been one of the foremost supporters of the Nicene Creed against the heresy of Arius, whom he reportedly even slapped in the face during one session.

His relics are nowadays kept in Bari, Italy. They had been transferred (some say: stolen) from Myra in 1187 when southern Asia Minor was overrun by the Seldjuq Turks.

The icon of *Agios Nikólaos* in the *naós* (13) shows the saint in the traditional style as an elderly bearded man with a balding head. His right hand is raised in a blessing gesture; in the other hand he carries the Bible as a symbol of his responsibilities as a bishop. His hands as well as his halo are covered with sheet silver – a hint at his merits as an intercessor. The conspicuous stole around his shoulders, emblazoned with black crosses, is the *omophórion*, still nowadays worn by Orthodox bishops. The saint's name is inscribed above his head. – The icon is said to have been painted in 1909 by a monk on Mount Athos. As the church works had come to a standstill, a distinguished resident of Kokkari kept it in his private home for three decades.

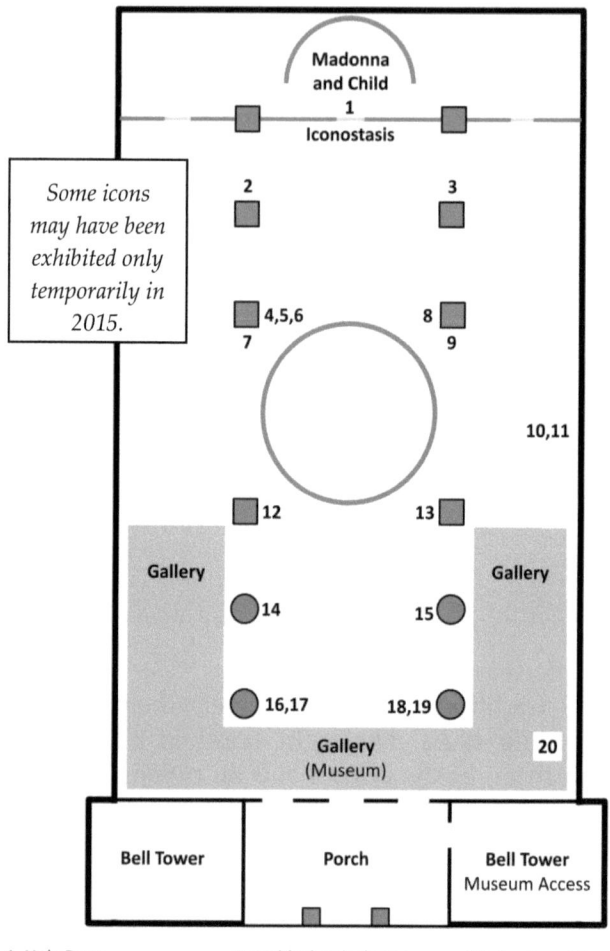

Some icons may have been exhibited only temporarily in 2015.

Madonna and Child
1
Iconostasis

2

3

4,5,6
7

8
9

10,11

12

13

Gallery

Gallery

14

15

16,17

18,19

20

Gallery
(Museum)

Bell Tower

Porch

Bell Tower
Museum Access

1 Holy Door
2 Ag. Giórgios of Samos
3 Ag. Fanourios
4 Pulpit
5 Ag. Konstantínos + Eléni
6 Holy Mary
7 Ag. Eleuthérios

8 Archbishop's throne
9 Ag. Kyrylýmpos
10 Holy water
11 Christ's symbolic grave
12 Ag. Pandeleímon
13 Ag. Nikólaos
14 Ag. Anna

15 Ag. Fanoúrios
16 Dormition of Holy Mary
17 Samos Saints
18 Ag. Nikólaos
19 Ag. Sozon (?)
20 Candle compartment

...

The marble pedestal of the Nicholas icon is inscribed "1939". Numerous votive gifts have been donated by thankful individuals whose invocations have been answered.Various other items deserve special attention:

- The symbolic grave of Jesus Christ (11).

- The silver sheeted icon of the Dormition of the *Panagía* from 1846 (16).

- The icon of *Agios Lefthérios*, a.k.a. *Elefthérios* (7). As the votive gifts suggest, he is probably the saint to turn to when a young man or woman is on the search for a good spouse. Again the right forearm and hand are covered with sheet silver, as well as the halo.

- The gilded double-headed eagle below this icon (7), with the sceptre, the orb and the crown. This was the symbol of the Byzantine Empire in the Middle Ages, and has been continued as the symbol of the Greek-Orthodox church. When displayed in a flag, the eagle is shown black on a golden (actually yellow) field.

- The countless *kathísmata* (choir stalls) all around the walls, each of them bought or rented by a member of the congregation whose name is pinned to the back.

- The intricate piece of furniture to keep burning candles safe (20).

- The many colourful frescos on the walls and especially in the cupola with its mystical light.

- From the porch a staircase in the clock tower leads to the spacious gallery above the rear of the nave and the side aisles.

The gallery accommodates a small local museum that has been gathered by *Pápa Giórgos*.

Additional information

The feast of *Agios Nikólaos* on December 6 includes the traditional *giórti* meal. –

The saint is invoked for many different reasons, but is most famous as the protector of sailors and fishermen. No wonder he is popular all along the coasts not only of Greece, but of many other countries.

Because of his role as the patron of seafaring people, a connection to the ancient Greek god of the seas, Poseidon, has occasionally been suggested.

Nicholas and his Look-Alikes

In Western Christianity Nicholas of Myra is one of the most popular saints in the Catholic camp. But on the Protestant side he also receives more than just friendly attention – especially children love him as a secret gift-bringer. In this role he is known in the Netherlands as *Sinterklaas*, in the USA as *Santa Claus* or just *Santa*.

In Westphalia, the author's home region, the children used to look forward in early December to the *Stutenkerl*, a pastry baked of sweet leavened dough in the form of a manikin with raisin buttons and a white clay pipe. When *St. Nikolaus* appeared in person to reward good children, he was often accompanied by black *Knecht Ruprecht*, "Servant Rupert" with the menacing birch rod.

The figures of *Father Christmas* in the USA or *Grandfather Frost* in Russia are secular counterparts. A modern myth holds that the old man with the white beard, clad in a red cloak, is an invention of the Coca-Cola promoters. But those producers of sugary soda pop just jumped on the bandwagon of an Old World tradition of ever so many centuries. Ho ho ho!

4. Άgios Athanásios & Tímios Stavrós
(St. Athanasius & Holy Cross), cemetery chapel

N037°46.697' E026°53.243' // 3m // map ▷ p. 144

The present-day cemetery at the south side of the beach road surrounds a dual chapel. The aisle to the left is dedicated to St. Athanasios, the one to the right to the Holy Cross. The interior of both aisles is well-tended and neat, so as to receive the mourners. In addition there is a spacious porch resting on three columns where the congregation may gather. A close look at the columns and some blocks of stone that are lying around will discover architectural relics from centuries ago.

Άγιος Αθανάσιος Αλεξανδρείας (Αθανάσιος ο Μέγας)

St. Athanasios of Alexandria, also known as "Athanasios the Great", was born some years before 300, and died in 373. His name *Athanásios*, "the Immortal", reflects the belief that the dead will rise to eternal life on doomsday, redeemed by Jesus Christ's death at the Holy Cross.

The saint grew up in Alexandria, Egypt, where his education combined Greek learning and study of the Holy Scriptures. As the secretary of Patriarch Alexander of Alexandria, Athanasios accompanied him to the First Council of Nicaea and became one of the most ardent exponents of the doctrine of the Holy Trinity against Arianism. He may even have had some influence on the wording of the Nicene Creed (▷ p. 68). In 328 he became Patriarch of Alexandria himself and continued to fight against heresies and schisms. His explosive character earned him many ecclesiastical and political enemies: Five times he was sent into exile by an emperor, some more times he had to flee from Alexandria to save his life. But he himself could be an inexorable adversary of any suspected heathen or heretic opposition in his zeal for the purity of the faith.

Because of his theological writings Athanasios is counted among the Church Fathers. He is also known for a letter from the year 367 which contains the first listing of the twenty-seven books of the New Testament as it is known today.

The saint was originally buried in Alexandria, but his remains were later transferred to Venice in Italy.

Ύψωσις του Τίμιου Σταυρού

The feast called "Elevation of the Holy Cross" commemorates the rediscovery of the Holy Cross by St. Helena, the mother of Emperor Constantine the Great, in 325.

The legend says that she came to Jerusalem in order to search for traces of Jesus Christ's life and death. Under the temple of the Roman goddess Venus that covered the hill of Golgotha a tomb was laid open. Inside, three wooden crosses were found, accompanied by Pontius Pilate's inscription: "Jesus of Nazareth, King of the Jews". But only one of them could be the true cross, the others had to be those of the two thieves crucified on either side of Christ. So a test was agreed upon: One cross after the other was laid on a sick woman. With the first and the second cross nothing happened, but when the third cross touched her she became immediately well. Even a dead man was revived that way. As a large crowd of people was present, the third cross was held up high for everybody to worship.

Emperor Constantine ordered a basilica to be built on the very place. It still exists today: the Church of the Holy Sepulchre or, as the Orthodox Church calls it, the *Naós tis Anastáseos*, "Church of the Resurrection".

According to tradition St. Helena's "True Cross" was soon split into more and more fragments. In the course of the centuries churches and convents all over the Christian world have claimed to own a particle of the Holy Cross, often the destination of a pilgrimage. The largest known fragment, slightly less than one cubic decimetre (i.e. a cube of 4 inches side length), is said to be preserved in the monastery of *Koutloumousíou* on Mount Athos.

Additional information

St. Athanasios is invoked as a helper against headaches. In the Orthodox Church his feast is celebrated on January 18, in Western Christianity on May 2.

The feast of *Tímios Stavrós* is celebrated on September 14 as a holy day of strict fasting and repentance. In Western Christianity it is also called "Exaltation of the Holy Cross".

If the cemetery around the double chapel appears quite small, this may be explained by the custom of re-using a grave after about half a dozen years. Even so, it cannot be denied that the site looks quite cramped.

The whole cemetery compound is taken care of by the local community, with special support for the chapels by several neighbours.

Chapels close to the Village

5. Panaítsa (Holy Mary) in Taliáni

N037°46.637' E026°53.060' // 6m // map ▷ p. 144

By-name: *Zoodóchos Pigí* ("life-giving spring").

The chapel, dedicated to the *Panagía*, the "All Holy" Virgin Mary, Mother of God, is perhaps the smallest of the chapels around Kokkari, but it is certainly one of the most beautiful. It really deserves its affectionate nickname *Panaítsa*, "little Mary".

Situated in the *Taliáni* neighbourhood, it is taken care of by the *Stavráki-Papourtzí* family, who have made it a real gem by a recent renovation.

The approach is somewhat uncomfortable because it requires a short walk along the Kokkari bypass. The entrance is dominated by the bell pillars and opens into a tiny forecourt like a flower garden. The position of the door in the side wall is an unusual but suitable solution.

Ζωοδόχος Πηγή

The old legend of the "Life-giving Spring" says that in 450 a Roman soldier called Leo Marcellus was passing a grove outside the walls of Constantinople when he met a blind man who had lost his way and was thirsty. So Leo looked around to find some water. Suddenly he heard a female voice leading him to a spring in the grove and telling him not only to fetch the water, but also to take some of the mud to put on the blind man's eyes. And, as the voice had predicted, the man immediately regained his sight.

Leo was to become the Byzantine Emperor Leo I in 457. He attributed the voice to Holy Mary, and ordered a magnificent church to be built on the site. Very soon the well became famous for its miraculous cures, and by the intercession of the *Theótokos*, the Mother of God, even resurrections of the dead came about – hence the name "Life-giving Spring".

Additional information

The inside of the building is kept immaculately clean, apparelled with white lace curtains and adorned with fresh flowers. The floor is covered with a hand-woven rag rug, whereas under the well-proportioned rafters a luxuriant gilded chandelier catches the eye. Perhaps there is a connection to the memorial tablet "Nicholas Michael Perris" († 2008)?

The byname *Zoodóchos Pigí* is illustrated in an icon: It shows the Madonna with the child on her arm, sitting on a marble basin from which the "water of life" pours down onto the world. The cross reference to the traditional baptismal font is obvious.

The feast of *Zoodóchos Pigí* is celebrated on "Bright Friday", the Friday after Easter, with a liturgical service in the afternoon, or on the following day.

6. Agía Triáda (Holy Trinity) in Triáda

N037°46.528′ E026°53.258′ // 20m // map ▷ p. 145

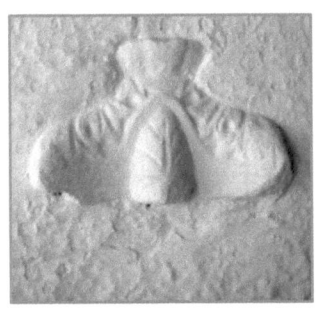

The chapel is reported to be 150 to 200 years old. According to local sources, it was erected on antique foundations, and was secretly used as a school in former times. Originally it had reportedly been crowned by a cupola, but owing to humidity the construction had to be replaced. Nevertheless the high vault above the narrow nave is still impressive. Above the gable there is a bell turret.

The age-worn relief on the right side of the front is a traditional sculpture of the Holy Spirit as a dove descending from heaven. Unfortunately the head of the sculpture has been destroyed, so it takes some fantasy to recognize the symbol.

The theological doctrine of the Holy Trinity, worked out by the early Church Fathers, was authoritatively formulated by the Council of Nicaea in 325. The Nicene Creed confirms what already the first Christians had confessed: "We believe in one God, the Father Almighty ... and in one Lord Jesus Christ, the Son of God ... and in the Holy Ghost."

Additional information

The iconostasis with only two icons looks very austere, but there is some nice though unobtrusive stucco work. The icon on the right shows the Holy Trinity: the Father, the Son, and the Holy Spirit, or Holy Ghost. Such icons are quite rare, because the Second Council of Nicaea (787) excluded the representation of God the Father in icons on principle, arguing that He is invisible and  cannot be depicted. And that the Holy Spirit could not be represented at all was considered self-evident.

Nonetheless the icon in this chapel presents God the Father as an old man with a grey beard and a halo with three characteristic outgrowths, together with Jesus Christ as a young man with a book, viz. the Holy

Gospel, and with the Holy Spirit hovering above them in the likeness of a dove.

In the Greek-Orthodox calendar, the feast of Holy Trinity is celebrated on Pentecost Monday, seven weeks after Easter.

The feast starts on Pentecost Sunday with an evening liturgy in the handsomely decorated chapel, followed by the preparation of the traditional *giortí* meal. On Monday morning the liturgy is held at 8 o'clock, and afterwards the *giortí* meal is shared.

The chapel is taken care of by the *Tserépas* family. –

The veneration of the Holy Trinity is closely inter-woven with the sign of the cross. There is an interesting difference between Eastern and Western Christianity in the way the sign of the cross is performed. Most Roman Catholics, for example, will use their open right hand to touch the forehead, the lower chest, the left and the right shoulder. A Greek Orthodox will bring together the thumb, index, and middle finger of his right hand, thus symbolizing the Holy Trinity, and press the other two fingers to the palm. He will also start with the forehead and the lower chest, but continue to the right shoulder first, before moving on to the left one.

7. Metamórfosis (Transfiguration) in Sotíros

N037°46.360' E026°53.616' // 25m // map ▷ p. 145

Although the chapel is quite close to the village, it is well hidden. It can only be reached by the narrow road that goes up behind the football ground south of the bypass.

The "Transfiguration of the Saviour" is reported in the Gospels (Matthew 17, Mark 9, Luke 9) as follows:

Jesus took his closest disciples Peter, James and John with him to the top of a mountain. Suddenly he was transfigured before them: "His face shone like the sun, and his clothes became as white as the light." Then Moses and the prophet Elijah appeared, and Jesus began to talk with them. At first the disciples were dazzled; then Peter offered to build three shelters for Jesus and the two prophets. He was interrupted by a voice from above saying: "This is my Son, whom I love; with him I am well pleased. Listen to him!" The disciples were stunned and fell to the ground. When Jesus touched them and they looked up, Elijah and Moses had disappeared. On their way down he told Peter, James and John not to speak about their experience until he would have risen from the dead – an admonition that they failed to understand at the time.

Additional information

The chapel's architectural style is quite sober. The iconostasis under the high vault is dark wood. The Transfiguration icon may not be very inspiring, but on the left is a notable icon of the birth of Holy Mary.

The feast *Metamórfosis tou Sotíros* ("Transfiguration of the Saviour") is celebrated on August 6, with a liturgy and the sharing of the traditional *giortí* meal, however with chick peas instead of meat. –

The chapel was reconstructed (ανοικολομηθη) in 1932, as a commemorative plaque outside indicates. The *Exoklísia* says this was in 1936, and adds that it was made possible by a donation from *Ioánnis Elissavítis*. Today the edifice is taken care of by the *Zográfos* family. In September 2014 it was under renovation.

The name of the small neighbourhood is also *Sotíros,* derived from the chapel.

8. Ἅgioi Paraskeví & Dimítrios (St. Paraskevi & St. Demetrius) inside ΔΕΗ power station

N037°46.518′ E026°54.005′ // 14m // map ▷ p. 145

This is one of the most interesting chapels in the Kokkari area because of its dual layout, with two aisles alongside each other, like its cemetery counterpart (▷ p. 60). Unfortunately it is situated inside the compound of the *ΔΕΗ* electicity works, so it is normally out of reach for the public.

One of the aisles is dedicated to *Agía Paraskeví*, the other to *Agios Dimítrios* (▷ p. 75, ▷ p. 101).

The feast of *Agía Paraskeví* is celebrated on July 26, and the authors of the *Exoklísia* assert that there is the traditional *giortí* meal. So this might be a chance to have a look at the otherwise inaccessible chapels. Whether a similar feast is held on the day of *Agios Dimítrios* (October 26) is a matter that could not be ascertained.

The chapels are taken care of by the personnel of the *ΔEH* workshops, who make it their pride to keep them in good shape.

Chapels in the South-Eastern Outskirts

The best access to this area is by the lane near the petrol station on the road to *Vathí* (Samos town), 100 metres beyond the junction of the main road and the bypass.

9. Panaítsa (Holy Mary) in Lagáda

N037°46.160′ E026°53.845′ // 117m // map ▷ p. 146

By-name: *Zoodóchos Pigí* ("life-giving spring").

This chapel in the *Lagáda* neighbourhood, with its bell turret above the gable, but without a bell, and with an old-fashioned low vault, is dedicated to the *Panagía*, the "All-Holy" Virgin Mary, Mother of God. It is also known as *Panaítsa*, "little Mary".

Two *Zoodóchos Pigí* icons show the Madonna with the child on her arm, sitting on a marble basin from which the "water of life" pours down onto the world (▷ p. 66).

The feast *Zoodóchos Pigí* is celebrated on Bright Friday, the Friday after Easter. On the eve people come together at the chapel where the traditional *giortí* meal is prepared. The chapel is taken care of by the *Tsivanáki* and *Iatroú* families.

Before leaving, take a look at the modern painting of the Last Supper above the exit. Has the painter taken some local men as his models? Likewise the waiter and the waitress relocate the scene in a Greek tavern, as it were.

10. Panagía (Holy Mary) in Lemós

N037°46.265' E026°53.938' // 66m // map ▷ p. 146

By-name: *Zoodóchos Pigí* ("life-giving spring").

This chapel in the *Lemós* neighbourhood on the way up to *Vígles* is dedicated to the *Panagia*, the "All-Holy" Virgin Mary, Mother of God. It is situated in a quiet cypress grove and was built in 1908 according to an inscription above the door. The column stumps, one at each side of the front, may go back to an earlier chapel in this location, or even to an antique place of worship.

The interior is unpretentious, but the ceiling with the rafters gives it a warm colour. The commemorative plaque in the iconostasis translates as follows: "The

renovation of the chapel took place in 2003 in memory of Andrea Lymberi. Dedicated by Simon Rekk."

The feast *Zoodóchos Pigí* is celebrated on Bright Friday, the Friday after Easter (▷ p. 66.)

The chapel is taken care of by the *Gékis* and *Chatzinikoláos* families.

11. Agía Paraskeví (St. Paraskevi) in Vígles

N037°45.788′ E026°54.318′ // 157m // map ▷ p. 146

Situated in the *Vígles* neighbourhood, positioned on a spacious plinth, and accompanied by a kind of belfry, the chapel is one of the most impressive specimens in the Kokkari area. From the stone bench under the porch, a fantastic view opens across some lower hills towards the *Karvoúnis* and *Lazárou* peaks.

Αγία Παρασκευή, παρθένα και μάρτυρας

St. Paraskeví, "Virgin and Martyr", suffered her martyrdom about 170 AD, possibly on the banks of the river Acheron near the Monastery of *Agía Paraskeví* in Thesprotia, Epirus. Her name means "Friday" – and the legend says she was actually born on a Friday. Or is the name a reference to the original meaning of the Greek word παρασκευή, "preparation", in this case preparation for the Lord's Day?

Born near Rome to Christian parents, she was a well-educated young woman ("well-prepared": another cue as to the name?). But she renounced marriage, sold her inheritance, and began to travel, preaching the gospel and healing the invalid wherever she went.

Once, when she had returned to Rome, she was denounced to Emperor Antoninus Pius. Neither threats nor temptations could change her mind, so she was subjected to tortures. When even in a mixture of boiling oil and tar she remained unscathed, the emperor approached the cauldron, only to be blinded immediately by the hot steam. But Paraskevi healed him in the name of Jesus Christ. Antoninus henceforward stopped the persecution of the Christians.

However, under his successor the persecution resurged. On one of her missionary travels Paraskevi was again arrested and submitted to tortures without avail. Eventually she was beheaded. Her remains were later transferred to Constantinople.

Additional information

In the summer of 2014 the pink coloration of the iconostasis was replaced by a chaste white. In the icon, St. *Paraskeví* is depicted traditionally as an earnest-looking young woman, veiled with a dark cloak. In one hand she holds a cross, in the other a cauldron, from whose interior two eyes gaze as if in terror.

St. Paraskevi's feast is celebrated on July 26. There is an evening liturgy on the day before, and the *giortí* meal is prepared. On the day itself a large number of people are present.

The chapel is taken care of by the *Gékis* family. –

The help of St. Paraskevi is invoked by people who suffer from diseases or injuries, especially by the blind and by those afflicted with eye ailments. In Western

Christianity her veneration has never gained a foot-hold, although her name, spelt "Parasceva", is not unknown. Her role as the patron saint of good eyesight is confided to St. Odile of Alsace.

12. Ágios Dimítrios (St. Demetrius) in Vígles

N37°45.788′ E26°54.685′ // 175m // map ▷ p. 146

The chapel in the *Vígles* neighbourhood is not easy to find behind the ruins of an old settlement. Where the overgrown cart track ends, you must detect the foot-path to the left and then to the right, however indistinct it may seem. You will be rewarded by a breathtaking view towards the Ambelos mountain massif.

The building itself is simple. A special feature is a beam across the room in front of the iconostasis; it stabilises the walls and also carries the lamps. For more information on St. Demetrius ▷ p. 101.

The saint's feast is on October 26. The chapel is taken care of by the *Theodóros* family.

13. Panagía (Holy Mary) in Vígles

N037°45.730' E026°54.790' // 186m // map ▷ p. 146

By-name: *Isódia tis Theotókou* ("Entry of the Birth-giver to God"), in Western Christianity known as the Presentation of the Virgin Mary at the Temple.

Although it seems as if this remote little chapel can only be reached by traversing some cultivated ground, there is actually a footpath: From the broad breach in the low hedge you want to turn left in order to walk round the vineyard on your right. The chapel walls are rough stone, and must have been repaired recently.

The Presentation of Holy Mary to the Temple in Jerusalem is not reported in the Gospels, but in the apocryphal "Gospel of St. James":

Mary's parents, Joachim and Anne, had been childless for many years. Childlessness was seen as a sign of God's displeasure, so Joachim eventually fasted and prayed in the desert for forty days, until angels appeared to him and also to his wife, promising them a child.

It was believed that a child born to an elderly mother who had given up hope was destined for great things. So, when Mary was born, the parents vowed to dedicate her to a god-fearing life. When she was twelve – other versions say: at the age of three – they took her to the Temple in Jerusalem to be educated there. In this way, so the legend suggests, she came to be prepared for her role as the Mother of God.

Additional information

Twice in 2014 the author was welcomed inside by a curious though wary little lizard, which looked down from the bearing of the rafters on the wall.

Most of the chapel's interior has been renovated, but the cobwebs betray a perfunctory supervision. Several of the icons exhibit a modern style, e.g. *Agios Nektários*, but one age-old painting has been preserved in the iconostasis. It is quite inconspicuous because the colours are scaled off or faded. It is painted on some unusual material – not on a flat rectangular wooden panel, but on a thin semi-circular slab of ceramics or something similar.

A closer look at the painting reveals the interior of a temple – the Temple of Jerusalem, to be sure. The High Priest is standing on the right, and a child, Holy Mary, is kneeling before him. Her parents, identified by their halos, are standing to the left of a white object in the centre.

The photo has been edited to emphasize the white object in the centre.

For this white object, shaped like a chalice, no plausible explanation is at hand. There seems to be nothing similar in other icons of the scene. Considering the location in the Temple of Jerusalem, it should have a distinct ritual meaning. The Showbread Table? The Altar of Burnt Offering? Or perhaps a coarse outline of the Brazen Sea, a.k.a. Molten Sea, a large brass basin in the forecourt of the Temple used by the priests for ritual cleaning? In this case it would introduce into the icon a symbolic overtone of purity – a traditional predicate of the Virgin Mary.

According to the Biblical report on the Temple of Solomon (1 Kings 7, 23-26), the Brazen Sea looked like a huge cup or a lily blossom, about 5 metres in diameter and 2.5 metres high, and with a capacity of about 90 cubic metres. It rested on twelve life-sized oxen of the same material, so that the rim may have been at least 4 metres from the ground. It is not quite clear if the cleaning ceremony of the priests meant the full immersion of the body, or only washing their hands and feet, as prescribed in Exodus 30, 17-21. In either case it is not very probable that this was done from the rim, or by plunging in. More likely there was some sort of overflow to wash or bathe in.

These details disclose an unexpected crosslink to the way the *Zoodóchos Pigí* icons depict Holy Mary, Mother of God (▷ p. 67)! And there may also be a connection to the baptismal font. –

The feast *Isódia tis Theotókou* is celebrated on November 21. The chapel is taken care of by the *Theodóros* family.

The *Exoklísia* authors call this chapel *Panagía Spilianí*. However, three sign posts in the *Lagáda* and *Pournára* neighbourhoods indicate quite clearly that this name designates the *Panagía* chapel described on p. 86.

14. Ágios Ioánnis Pródromos (St. John Baptist) in Vígles

N037°45.677' E026°54.790' // 191m // map ▷ p. 146

Vígles is a quiet neighbourhood to the south-east of Kokkari. Two tall cypresses guard the access to a simple quarry stone chapel which commemorates the Beheading of St. John the Forerunner, a.k.a. John the Baptist. An inscription above the door reads "1914", indicating that the chapel was probably built that year. The walls are rough stone, but each window is nicely framed with red brick. The simple fibre cement roof protects the flat wooden ceiling inside. The bell is fastened to one of the cypresses.

Άγιος Ιωάννης Πρόδρομος

According to the Gospels St. John "the Forerunner", i.e. the Baptist, was the cousin of Jesus Christ (Mark 6; Matthew 14). As a young man he withdrew into the barren mountains between Jerusalem and the Dead Sea, wearing coarse garments of camel's hair and eating locusts and wild honey. Later he started preaching, speaking of himself as "a voice of one crying out in the desert: Prepare the way of the Lord." Hence his by-name *Pródromos*, "Forerunner".

Many people came to the bank of the River Jordan to repent and to be baptized by the new prophet. Among these, also Jesus set out for the Jordan to be baptized.

This culminated in the moment when a voice from heaven denominated him as the Son of God.

Some months later, when St. John accused King Herod Antipas of his incestuous marriage to Herodias, he was imprisoned. One day Herod celebrated a feast, and when his stepdaughter Salome had danced before him and his guests, he offered her a favour. Irresolute, she asked her mother Herodias, who advised her to request St. John's head.

Additional information

The wooden iconostasis in rich dark brown displays a collection of icons in a similar style. The patron saint's icon shows quite drastically how the executioner hands over St. John's head on a platter to a young girl (Salome). The corpse is lying on the floor, and in the background a woman (Herodias) is gloating at the prophet's death.

The feast of the Decapitation of *Ioánnis Pródromos* is celebrated on August 29 as a holy day of strict fasting. Yet the *giortí* meal is shared, albeit in a modified composition: chick peas instead of meat.

The chapel is taken care of by the *Theodóros* family.

Profítis Ilías on the Hill Crest

Following the cart track beyond St. John's chapel and keeping left at the next junction, a *Profítis Ilias* chapel can soon be seen on the right, perched on a steep hill crest. It does not actually belong to the parish of Kokkari, but its location is worth the detour. From up there one also has a good view of the Pyramid Mountain further east.

Chapels in the Southern Outskirts

The shortest access takes you from St. Nicholas parish church to the dyke of the *Giánnides* rivulet, crossing the Kokkari bypass at the water tap with the windmill. Ten minutes further on, where the cart track starts to ascend, look for the footpath branching off on the left. Passing below *Profítis Ilías* (▷ p. 93), the *monopáti* eventually reaches the cart track to *Mytilinií*.

15. Panagía (Holy Mary) in Pournára

N037°45.357′ E026°53.887′ // 258m // map ▷ p. 145

By-name: *Isódia tis Theotókou* ("Entry of the Birth-giver to God"), in Western Christianity known as the Presentation of the Virgin Mary at the Temple.

This is the only chapel that is located outside the basin of Kokkari, just beyond the watershed towards the village *Mytilinií*, in a neighbourhood whose name is alternately given as *Pournára* (*Prinára*?), *Katsélos* or *Spilianí*. Perhaps these three neighbourhoods converge at this point.

The "Spiliani" sign posts in the *Lagáda* and *Pournára* neighbourhoods prove that this is the real *Panagía Spilianí*, although the *Exoklísia* attaches this name also to a chapel in *Vígles* (▷ p. 79). The word *spiliá* means "cave", "grotto", but there seems to be nothing of the sort around. Neither is there any sign of a link to *Moní Spilianí*, a monastery in a cave near Pythagorio.

The simple building is easily overlooked because it ducks down modestly under some cypresses below the *Pournára* cart track. The door with its nice carving on the inside swings out and is kept shut by a column stump. It obviously replaces a previous door with inside hinges.

For background information on the *Isódia tis Theotókou* ▷ p. 80.

The iconostasis under the simple ceiling contains a standard depiction of the Presentation at the Temple as well as a remarkable icon of St. Fanourios (top right).

The feast, celebrated on November 21, is very popular. People arrive in large numbers to share the traditional *giortí* meal. – The chapel is taken care of by the *Geralídon* family.

16. Ágios Ioánnis Apóstolos (St. John Evangelist) in Karás

N037°45.528′ E026°53.501 // 214m // map ▷ p. 145

Situated in the *Karás* neighbourhood, the chapel is not easy to find. The best access is from the "Mytilinií Pass": When coming up from Kokkari, you take the cart track to the left along the ridge, and after 200 metres you turn left again, down into the valley for another 500 metres. Then the chapel will be on your left behind a fence. Unfortunately it lies within a private compound, and often the gate is closed.

Άγιος Ιοάννισ Απόστολος

From early Christianity the tradition has been handed on that John the Apostle, the "disciple whom Jesus loved", the author of the Fourth Gospel, and the author of the Book of Revelation are one and the same person. He owes his Greek by-name *Theólogos* to the first line of the Gospel that is attributed to him: "In the beginning was the Word, and the Word was with God, and the Word (*lógos*) was God (*theós*)."

John was a close relative to Jesus, one of his first disciples, and one of the twelve apostles. He was sitting next to Jesus at the Last Supper (John 14) and witnessed the crucifixion on Golgotha, where Jesus commended his mother Mary to his care (John 19). After Pentecost he was one of the leaders of the Christian congregation in Jerusalem.

When Holy Mary had died, his missionary travels took him to Ephesus, where he is reported to have written the Fourth Gospel and – while exiled on the island of Patmos – also the *Apokálypsi*, the Book of Revelation. According to legends, he was submitted to several tortures during a persecution of the Christians. But neither a cup of deadly poison nor an immersion in boiling oil could do him any harm. He is believed to be the only apostle who died a natural death.

Additional information

The very dark wood of the ceiling contrasts with the plain white walls. The icon of St. John depicts him as an old man sitting in a cave. Obviously the reference is to the Cave of the Apocalypse on Patmos, where the last book of the New Testament is believed to have been written. The old man has just turned his head over his right shoulder, as if torn from his thoughts by an unexpected event; perhaps it is the moment reported at the beginning of the Book of Revelation (1:10): "I heard behind me a great voice, as of a trumpet", which marks the start of the vision. On the left, an angel is whispering into the saint's ear; on the right, his disciple Prochoros is preparing to write down the vision on a scroll. In the background a bunch of candles is dimly visible.

At first sight this icon resembles a frequent *Profítis Ilías* motive, namely the sojourn inside or in front of a cave (▷ p. 93). The similarity may be a means to draw a connection between two great prophets – one from the Old Testament, the other from the New Testament.

The main feast of the saint is celebrated on September 26. The chapel is taken care of by the *Vergínis* family, the owners of the estate, who are also in charge of the feast. Next to the chapel there is a tiny burial ground for the deceased of the family. –

Another by-name of the saint is *Ioánnis Thermástis*, from *thermós*, "hot", because he is invoked to heal malaria, the "hot fever".

17. Ágios Ioánnis Pródromos (St. John Baptist) in Giánnides

N037°45.847′ E026°53.132′ // 161m // map ▷ p. 145

Erroneously ascribed to *Agía Ekateríni* (St. Catherine) in some maps.

Situated at the upper end of the *Giánnides* valley, the chapel enjoys the most romantic location in the Kokkari back hills, surrounded by awe-inspiring trees, with a water basin nearby. The bell is tied to the branch of a tree.

Under the flat wooden ceiling the painting in the iconostasis shows the moment when the executioner has raised his sword to behead the saint. In the background of another icon at the wall on the right Salome is shown dancing, triumphantly raising the platter with the saint's head.

The feast of the Beheading of St. John the Forerunner is celebrated on August 29 (▷ p. 83). The chapel is taken care of by the *Kritikós* family.

18. ʹAgios Giórgios (St. George) in Giánnides

N037°45.922′ E026°53.098′ // 187m // ▷ map p. 145

The chapel, situated in the *Giánnides* neighbourhood, is a simple building that has virtually been out of function for a number of years. But although it has suffered from inadequate maintenance and the roof is on the verge of falling into disrepair, it is still worth a visit. In former times it must have had a vaulted roof, the traces of which can still be seen. But now there is a simple construction of beams and rafters. A particularly sturdy beam serves as the lintel above the low door.

In most icons St. George (▷ p. 102) is depicted as mounted upon a white horse and piercing the dragon

with his spear. He may be accompanied by St. Demetrius, who can be distinguished by his red or black horse.

Here, however, the painting in the iconostasis shows neither the dragon nor St. Dimitrios. Nevertheless St. George is identified by the inscription.

The feast of the saint is celebrated on April 23, or, if this date occurs before Easter, on Easter Monday. The chapel is looked after by the *Galánis* family, and there is hope that some refurbishment can be done.

19. Profítis Ilías (Prophet Elijah) in Giánnides

N037°46.190′ E026°53.180′ // 94m // map ▷ p. 144

The chapel is situated in the fore of the *Giánnides* neighbourhood, halfway up the hill. It is just a thirty minutes' walk from Kokkari using an old footpath (look out for the steps upwards on the right!), and offers a nice view of the village and the sea.

The lowest step to the small forecourt is awkwardly inscribed: "22-6-01 Φ.Κ." Despite some wear and tear, the date seems to refer to 2001 rather than to 1901, and may go back to a renovation in the year in question.

Before you approach the door, which is, against the usual layout, inserted in the right side wall, you may look down at the slabs of the quarry stone forecourt, and up at the bell turret above the gable. And when you have left, do not forget to walk round to the north side to enjoy the scenic view.

Προφήτης Ηλίας

The prophet's name means "My God is Yahweh". As told in 1 Kings 17, Elijah came to the fore when Ahab, King of Israel, and his wife Jezebel promoted the cult of the Canaanite idol Baal. Elijah fiercely warned them that God would send years of terrible drought as a punishment. Then he fled to the barren lands east of the Jordan. While hiding in a grotto by the brook Cherith, he was provided with bread by ravens, as God had promised him.

After returning to stand his ground in many years of confrontation with Ahab, Jezebel and their son Ahaziah, the prophet and his disciple Elisha peregrinated to the Jordan (2 Kings 2). When Elijah's mantle touched the water, the waves divided, so that they could cross the river on dry ground. As soon as they had reached the other bank, a chariot of fire appeared and took Elijah in a whirlwind upwards and out of sight. Elisha was distressed and rent his clothes. But then he saw that Elijah's mantle had fallen to the ground and picked it up. On his way back across the river the waves divided once again at the touch of the mantle, and this was taken as a sign that Elisha was to be Elijah's successor.

Additional information

The iconostasis contains a painting of a flaming chariot with four fiery-red horses and whirling wheels disappearing in the clouds. While Elijah is lifted up towards heaven, his mantle is falling down to be picked up by Elisha.

Next to the door a distinctly modern icon shows the scene of the raven delivering in his beak a piece of bread to the starving prophet.

Like the other prophets Elijah is considered a saint by the Orthodox Christianity, but is traditionally referred to under the label *profítis*. The feast is celebrated on July 20, including the preparation and sharing of the *giortí* meal. The chapel is taken care of by the *Vergíni* family. –

According to Kokkarian *P. Mirsiádis*, the ruins in the vicinity of the chapel were used as field lodges in the summer well into the second half of the 20th century. Look out for the oven! –

In Greece the chapels dedicated to *Profítis Ilías* seem to be among the most frequent, second only to those devoted to the *Panagía*. Very often they are positioned on top of a hill or mountain (e.g. on *Karvoúnis*), which may be a hint at the prophet's ride towards the sky – a miracle that has ever since fired people's fantasy.

It has occasionally been suggested that the cult of the sun god *Ílios* (Helios) was a predecessor. This hypothesis is based on the report of the chariot of fire, and also on the striking similarity in the pronunciation of the two names. But in Antiquity it was an exception for Helios shrines to be installed on mountain tops.

Another hypothesis argues that some Elijah locations may have taken over cult sites of Zeus, as either of them is associated with mountains and with powers over thunder, lightning, rain, and wind. Even a confirmed Zeus sanctuary on Mount Olympos is reported to be dedicated to *Profítis Ilías* nowadays.

Chapels in the South-Western Outskirts

Access by the lane at *Mylos Beach* hotel. At the cart track fork (1 km or 15 mins. upwards) keep left for the *Panaítsa* chapel (below), but turn right for the others.

20. Panaítsa (Holy Mary) in Dendriás

N037°46.343' E026°52.917' // 84m // map ▷ p. 144

By-name: *Kímisis tis Theotókou* (Dormition of the "Birth-giver to God", i.e. of the Mother of God). Like some other *Panagía* chapels, it is nicknamed *Panaítsa*, "little Mary".

In some maps the chapel is erroneously ascribed to *Agía*

Fotíni. This saint is traditionally identified with the Samaritan woman whom Jesus met at the well (John 4). She is usually depicted with a water jug. Her icon on the right of the iconostasis may have given rise to the misunderstanding mentioned above.

This *Panaítsa* is situated inconspicuously in the *Dendriás* neighbourhood, to the left of the cart track to *Mytilinií*.

A fresco of the Dormition scene (▷ p. 50) can be found in a niche. Eleven of the apostles are standing by, and in the foreground the dissevered hands of the disruptive *Antonios* can be recognised just below the hands of Holy Mary.

Additional information

The feast is celebrated on August 15. Whether it includes the traditional *giortí* meal at the site is not quite clear. The chapel is taken care of by some neighbouring families: *Kazóglou*, *Giánnis*, *Chalvatzís*, and *Kavéso*. –

The name *Dendriás*, from *déndro*, "tree", is said to refer to the many olive groves in the area. There are in fact some remarkably old olive trees in the chapel's vicinity.

21. Profítis Ilías (Prophet Elijah) in Aiogdítes

N037°46.218′ E026°52.563′ // 120m // map ▷ p. 144

Erroneously ascribed to *Ágios Geórgios* in some maps.

The chapel, situated only a minute off the itinerary to *Móni Vrondá* and *Kástro Louloudás*, has recently been renovated. The coarse masonry gives an idea of its age. The bright blue cupola, the bell turret and the small porch taken together suggest that the chapel may have a distinguished history. And it was indeed built in the

18th century to serve as the *metrópolis* (i.e. primal church) of the surrounding area, before the congregation of the *Panagía* in the village (▷ p. 46) was set up.

The foundation date is specified in a commemorative plaque in Greek and English, "Profitis Ilias. Built in 1786", with the Greek addition, "Kokkari, Samos. Dedicated by *Konstandínos Arvanítis*." The porch is somewhat constricted, but the interior offers a well-proportioned room on an almost square ground plan.

The inside of the cupola above the cross vault looks like grey dirt at first sight, but a closer inspection reveals the faint traces of a time-worn fresco – a feature which is unique among the Kokkari chapels.

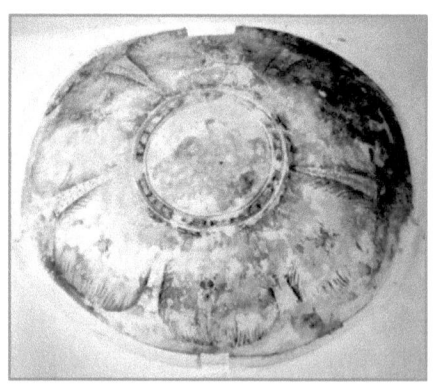

The painting in the iconostasis presents the scene in which the prophet is fed by a raven (▷ p. 93, with more information on the prophet).

Additional information

The feast of *Profítis Ilías* is celebrated on July 20. It includes the traditional *giortí* meal. The chapel is taken care of by the *Arvanítis* and *Mirsiádis* families.

The foundation date (1786) does not necessarily mean that *Profítis Ilías* is the oldest chapel in the Kokkari area. But it seems to have been the first with a self-contained congregation and possibly even a resident priest. And it is far and wide the only chapel with choir stalls, which indicate a stable congregation and regular services.

The implication of the location is that the neighbourhoods *Aiogdítes* and *Giánnides* must have been among the oldest settlements in the area, probably long before the village at the coast.

Aiogdítes is a particularly interesting case. The Yearbook 1875 of the Samos Hegemony allocates the κώμιον ("hamlet") to Vourliótes instead of Kokkari. The number of houses is given as 32, with 130 occupants – a surprising figure in comparison with today's marginal population. The Yearbook spells the name as Ἀγειο-γδύται, and also offers an explanation. It derives the name from the trade of the early inhabitants: αιγο-γδάρτες (αίγα, "goat"; γδάρτης, "skinner").

Today the name occurs on maps and sign posts in any combination of *ágio/aío* and *dítes/gdítes*. The component *dítes* is occasionally translated as "one who sees", resulting in the the combination "seer of the saint(s)". But this may be a benevolent etymology in retrospect. And *agiogdítes* – "skinner of the saint(s)", or less offensively, "scorner of the saint(s)" – seems more objectionable in the end than *aiogdítes*, "goat skinner".

To make things even more complicated, *Giakoúmis Amyrsónis*, the orchid gardener, has come up with an explanation of his own. Recalling how many times the offertory boxes of those remote chapels have been broken up end emptied, he dubs those thieves "skinners of the saints".

Anyway, while none of these hypotheses can be definitely confirmed, it should not be forgotten that goat breeding was a respectable trade. Goat or sheep skins as containers for water or wine were a staple means of transport in antiquity, in the Middle Ages, and even well into the early modern period. So, as there is really nothing insulting in the name, *Aiogdítes* has been chosen in this booklet to denote the neighbourhood.

22. Ágios Dimítrios (St. Demetrius) in Aiogdítes

N037°46.283' E026°52.402' // 171m // map ▷ p. 144

The chapel is situated high above Kokkari and offers a magnificent scenic view. On the hike upwards along the cart track, the bell turret

and the stately gable suddenly appear on the hillside to left. At the top of the access stairs, the tiny porch is an unexpected welcome. On a hot day it is a nice place to rest in the shade. Inside there is a low barrel vault.

Άγιος Δημήτριος της Θεσσαλονίκης, Μεγαλομάρτυρες

»St. *Dimítrios* of *Thessaloníki*, the Greatmartyr«, was born to pious Christian parents in Thessaloniki in 270. The young man is believed to have entered a military career. The legend says that in the year 306, during the persecution of Christians under the emperors Diocletian and Galerius, he was run through with spears.

In the Middle Ages he was chosen by the crusaders as their patron, together with St. George, and still today he is considered the patron of the soldiers.

Additional information

The name *Dimítrios* is originally derived from *Dímitra* (Demeter), the Greek goddess of agriculture and fertility. From this point of view his frequent appearance together with St. George ("the farmer") is no surprise.

In traditional icons St. Demetrius is presented either as a Roman foot soldier, or – often together with St. George – as a cavalryman riding a red or black horse. Here, in the painting in the iconostasis, he is on his own riding his mount. His spear is swung victoriously over a man lying on the ground, according to the legend a gladiator who had killed many Christians during a persecution.

The saint's feast is celebrated on October 26 and includes the liturgy as well as the traditional sharing of the *giortí* meal. The chapel is taken care of by the *Klóthos* family.

23. Ágios Geórgios (St. George) in Aiogdítes

N037°46.358′ E026°52.513′ // 100m // map ▷ p. 144

The location is somewhat remote in the lower reaches of the *Aiogdítes* neighbourhood and accessible only from above; so the *Profítis Ilías* chapel in *Aiogdítes* (▷ p. 97) is the best starting point.

Surrounded by a small plinth, *Agios Geórgios* has a bell turret in an unusual position, namely sideways from the roof ridge. Above the door there is a cross surrounded by an inscription; the upper line to the right of the cross seems to contain numerals: "1798"? The rest of the text is hardly recognizable und still waiting to be deciphered.

Άγιος Γεώργιος, Μεγαλομάρτυρες και Τροπαιοφόρος

The name *Geórgios* means "worker of the land", or in short "farmer".

St. George, »Great-martyr and Trophy-bearer«, is believed to have been born in Cappadocia during the late 3rd century, and to have grown up a half-orphan in Palestine. Like his father, a Roman officer who had died a martyr, he took up a brilliant military career. When Emperor Diocletian ordered a persecution of the Christians in 303, George confessed to being a Christian himself. The emperor tried in vain to make him recant, and in his frustration he had him tortured and eventually beheaded.

The popular legend of St. George and the Dragon was brought back from the East in the Middle Ages by the crusaders. It narrates how a monster chose for its lair a spring that provided a near-by heathen town with water. The horrified citizens found out that they could only lure the beast away from the spring if they offered it a daily human sacrifice, chosen by drawing lots.

One day the local princess was drawn, and everybody deplored her fate. At the very moment when the voracious dragon approached her, a travelling knight arrived on the scene: St. George. Protecting himself with the sign of the Cross, he attacked the monster and managed to slay it. The overjoyed citizens now converted to Christianity.

Additional information

Inside the wooden iconostasis, with its red curtains, is overarched by a barrel vault. The colourful St. George icon shows his fight with the dragon; from the background the desperate princess is watching.

The feast is celebrated on April 23, or, if this date occurs before Easter, on Easter Monday. It includes the liturgy as well as the *giortí* meal. The chapel is taken care of by the *Kipréou* and *Partsáfas* families. –

Incidentally the legend of St. George and the Dragon has a striking predecessor in the classic Greek myth of Perseus and his rescue of the princess Andromeda. –

The saint is one of the Fourteen Holy Helpers; he is invoked as a protector in times of war and plague, and also as the guardian of domestic animals.

St. George has gained additional fame as the patron of many countries and cities, in particular of England, as the white flag with the red St. George's Cross witnesses. The tradition originated in the 13th century, but the official breakthrough seems to have come in 1348 with the foundation of the Most Noble Order of the Garter ("Honi soit qui mal y pense"), whose emblem has been the red cross on a white background ever since.

Chapels in the Western Outskirts

Access either by the lane at the *Mylos Beach* hotel, turning right after 150 metres towards the Limp Mill Arch, or by the lane up to the hotels on the western hill.

24. Ágios Ioánnis Pródromos (St. John Baptist) in Pótami

N037°46.508′ E026°52.695′ // 58m // map ▷ p. 144

This is one of the outstanding chapels in the area of Kokkari, situated in a secluded place on a hillock behind the *Potámi* plain. After passing the archway of the "Limp Mill", a serpentine flight of stairs on the left ascends to a wide open space, surrounded by trees on three sides, and with an impressive view on the fourth side of the *Louloúdas* peaks.

The building itself is crowned by a bell turret above the gable. The front wall as well as the vault inside indicate the chapel's age and proudly proclaim the craftsmanship of the mason.

Additional information

The floor of the chapel is a special feature: a mosaic of countless pebbles.

The icon of St. John shows a bearded man holding an identical head on a platter – a traditional interpretation of the saint's beheading (▷ p. 83). Underneath, a collection of votive gifts shows that the "Forerunner" has successfully been asked for his intercession.

The chapel is taken care of by the *Amyrsónis* family.

The feast of the Decapitation of *Ioánnis Pródromos* is celebrated on August 29 as a holy day of strict fasting. This is why the recipe for the *giortí* meal has been modified to chick peas instead of meat. The liturgy on the day itself is held, according to the *Exoklísia* authors, by a priest sent from the Metropolitan in Samos town. Maybe in former times a monk came down from *Moní Vrondá*.

When the forecourt had to be overhauled some years ago, traces of graves were found underneath, which suggests that the chapel is among the oldest around. –

Like St. *Pandeleímonas*, the chapel belongs to the estate of the monastery *Panagía tis Vrondianí* (*Moní Vrondá*) in *Vourliótes* (▷ p. 110).

25. Ágios Pandeleímonas (St. Pantaleon) in Mána

N037°46.597' E026°52.335' // 53m // map ▷ p. 144

The chapel is situated unobtrusively in the picturesque setting of *Pigí Mána* (Mána Spring), with its age-old plane trees and its abundance of water, which fills the taps of Kokkari. The edifice is believed to have been built, or reconstructed, in the 19th century.

There is a bell turret on the roof, and a low vault plus an unusual pebble floor inside.

Άγιος Παντελεήμων, μεγαλομάρτυρας και γιατρός

St. Pandeléimon, the "Greatmartyr and Healer", suffered his martyrdom in Nicomedia in 303 AD. His parents had named him *Pantaléon*, "all like a lion", or in today's lingo: "mega lion". Having been educated as a physician, he soon became respected as the doctor who healed the poor, the persecuted, and the helpless free of charge, in the name of Jesus Christ. Some say his fame even spread to the heathen emperor Maximinian, who, unaware that the young man had

become a Christian, made him his personal physician.

Eventually some jealous competitors denounced him. In the emperor's court, Pantaleon refused to sacrifice to the pagan idols, but offered to enter a competition with his adversaries in their common professional field. So a man who had been paralyzed for many years was brought to the law court. The heathen physicians tried their skills in vain, whereas the saint healed the man by invoking the name of Jesus Christ. Maximinian was furious and ordered Pantaleon to be tortured. However, the saint remained untouched. Even the beasts in the circus did him no harm. Eventually the emperor sentenced him to death.

For the execution Pantaleon was tied to an olive tree, with his hands nailed to his head. While he was praying for his tormentors, one of the soldiers raised his sword to behead him – but the sword melted like wax, and a voice from above called the saint by a new name, *Pandeleímon*, the "All-merciful", summoning him to the Kingdom of Heaven. The soldiers, struck with terror, fell on their knees. St. *Pandeleímon* told them to rise and complete the execution. As soon as his head fell, the olive tree burst out with fruit.

The martyr's body was thrown into a fire, but it remained unharmed and was given a Christian burial. His head is preserved in a monastery on Mount Athos, or, as some say, on the island of Andros.

His help is invoked by people who suffer from diseases or injuries, and also by disabled persons. Perhaps he is also the secret helper of the olive farmers?

Additional information

In the icon, St. Pandeleimon is represented traditionally as a beardless young man with curly hair. In one hand he wields a lancet or a medicine spoon, in the other he carries a casket with several compartments, apparently to keep various medicines in. In other icons he may be depicted with his hands nailed to his head.

St. Pandeleimon's feast is celebrated on July 27, including the traditional *giortí* meal. It is considered the oldest and most prestigious of the Kokkari feasts, attracting participants from all over Samos. The chapel itself is taken care of by the *Amyrsónis* family – now in the fifth generation, according to G. *Amyrsónis*.

St. Pandeleímon belongs to the estate of the monastery *Panagía tis Vrondianí* (short: *Moní Vrondá*) in *Vourliótes*. Whether there are more points of contact could not be established. The fact that the main tributary to the waters of *Pigí Mána* has its source quite close to the monastery may be dismissed as insignificant. But the local tradition connects the early years of the convent to the upper Kokkari neighbourhoods (▷ p. 15). –

In Western Christianity the saint is known as St. Pantaleon, and has become one of the Fourteen Holy Helpers, the patron of doctors and midwives, as well as the protector of weeping children. In Italy he is supposed to grant lottery luck.

In Cologne, Germany, a church in Romanesque style dedicated to St. Pantaleon goes back to the 10th century and even a predecessor from the 9th. It contains the tomb of the Byzantine princess Theophanou († 991), who had become the wife of Emperor Otto II. She is renowned for her wise regency for her son Otto III after her husband's death.

26. Ágios Fanoúrios (St. Fanourios) in Paleokalíva

N037°47.013′ E026°52.418′ // 78m // map ▷ p. 144

The chapel looks down from a foothill high above the beaches of *Lemonákia* and *Tsamadoú*. The neighbourhood is called *Paleokalíva*, "old cottage", or *Tsamadoú* as well; it seems that the beach is rather named after the neighbourhood than vice versa.

Agios Fanoúrios is the largest of Kokkar's outlying chapels, and also the most recent. An icon of the saint in the centre of the nave is dated as 1999. The erection and endowment of the edifice owes much to the initiative and the support of several Kokkari families.

Before you enter by the spacious porch, enjoy the wide forecourt. It offers a stunning view of Kokkari's Long Beach, with the harbour cape, the village hill, and the imposing parish church St. Nicholas in the middle ground, and far out the mountains of Turkey as a backdrop.

Άγιος Φανούριος, Μεγαλομάρτυρας

Where and when St. Fanourios, the "Greatmartyr", suffered his martyrdom nobody knows. His name may be related to the Greek verb φανερώνω (*faneróno*, "reveal").

The legend goes back to 1522 when the island of Rhodes had been conquered by the Ottomans after a long siege. The survivors, whether Muslims or Christians, had to clear the rubble before the city could be rebuilt. In quite some depth a group of Turks hit on a chapel which contained some age-worn and badly damaged icons. Being Muslims, they carelessly threw them away as idols of the infidels. Some monks who had watched them from afar recovered the icons and were amazed to see that one of them looked as if it had been painted that very day. The inscription identified the young saint as Άγιος Φανούριος. Twelve scenes from the martyrdom of the same person were arranged around the central picture; in one of the tortures he was burnt with candles, in another he was standing inside the flames of a fire.

It did not take long before the saint whose icon had been so miraculously found proved to be a wonderworker himself. His fame spread when he appeared to three priests from Crete who had been sold into slavery but owed their liberation to the saint's intervention.

Additional information

The inside the chapel surprises by its high ceiling and the coloured upper windows. Two arches suggest a transept. The walls display colourful frescos in a contemporary style. The iconostasis of white stucco is adorned with tiny angels and five double-headed Byzantine eagles.

Alongside the Fanourios icon in the centre of the nave, a touching Madonna with her child catches the eye. Both icons show a remarkably modern style.

St. Fanourios himself can be represented in different ways. Mostly he appears as a very young man carrying a sword and a lighted candle (or a cross with a candle fixed to the top). Or he may be clad in a Roman soldier's armour, equipped with a lance or a sword. Or he may be standing in the midst of a fire with his arms raised in prayer. So it can be difficult to identify him at first sight in an icon. But in this case the traditional inscription in the top right corner of the painting confirms the saint's identity.

The chapel is taken care of by the *Papourtzís* and *Levisianós* families.

The feast of *Agios Fanoúrios* is celebrated on August 27. The festivities are very popular and attended by a large number of guests. On the evening before, a liturgy is held. It is followed by a cheerful sharing not only of *fanourópita* (see below), but also of beer and soft drinks, *souvláki* and sausages, all of them contributed by friendly donors. Meanwhile the traditional *giortí* meal is prepared, so that in the morning, after another liturgy, the traditional stew can be dished out. –

Remembering the mysterious revelation of the saint's icon, people invoke his help to find lost objects. When the object has turned up, they bake sweet bread rolls, the *"fanourópita"* ("Fanourios cake"), and share them with the poor, or at least with the family.

The following simple *fanourópita* recipe should be worth an attempt: "The pita is usually small and round and is made of pure flour, sugar, cinnamon, and oil. Mix, knead, put in a round cake form, and bake under medium temperature in the oven." You can of course find other, more elaborate recipes! –

In Western Christianity *Fanoúrios* has never been adopted as a saint. His role as the helper of the forgetful in search of lost or mislaid objects is ascribed to St. Anthony of Padua.

A Kiss on Wings

Once you have paid a reverential visit to *Agios Fanoúrios*, a nice surprise is waiting for you some 100 metres up the cart track (just below the country house on the right): The little arch framing a water tap is crowned by the relief of two kissing angels.

Angels they may be, but they are certainly beyond the age of innocent putti, aren't they?

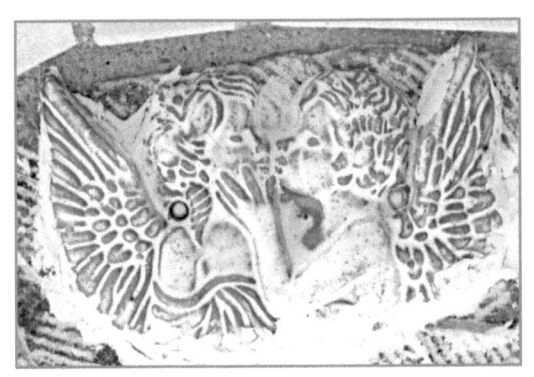

Kokkari's Secular Sights

The Community, the School, and the Well

Kokkari's school provides elementary education; for secondary education the children are shuttled to Samos Town. The local school compound is situated several hundred metres up the main street from the parish church. The complex was built in 1972, so the question arises where the local school had been before.

The answer is: In the heart of the village – a brown stone building next to *Panaítsa*, the old parish church. The two-sided stairs in the middle of the symmetric front lead to the main entrance. The interior has been partly rearranged, but the old ground plan of a school is still recognisable as you enter the corridor: one classroom on the left, another on the right, and a tiny compartment for the "senior teacher" in the background. The toilets must have been at the back of the school house.

The classroom on the left has been converted into two lengthy compartments to accommodate the community office, with the president residing in the first, and the secretary in the second. But on the right the old classroom can still be imagined in its original size, although it seems to have been renovated after the relocation of the school. It is now a sort of community hall.

During the occasional opening hours of the community office one may meet some local people waiting for an appointment with the president or the secretary. Those villagers who belong to the older generation can tell many tales of their school days, which used to take 6 years when they were young. The senior children's class was on the left, the juniors' on the right. In winter each classroom was heated by a stove; every child had to bring some firewood.

During those years when the growing number of pupils could no longer be crammed into the two classrooms, the youngest of them were taught next door in the *Panaítsa* church. The churchyard was anyway used as the playground during the recesses. –

Before the advent of tourism, as late as the 1960s, this quarter of Kokkari was its thriving heart, as Kokkari-born *V. Galánis-Moutáfis* vividly describes. Youngsters who were about to go out and meet their friends would say, "I'm going to the village", meaning an area with a radius of 50-odd metres around the *Panaítsa* and the school.

Today a considerable number of houses in this vicinity are deserted; several of them have fallen into disrepair. Of the few tiny shops only one seems to have survived: the *Pantopoleíon*, the "All-Shop" of the *Vogiátzis* family, founded in 1939, near the corner of the main road and *Odós Psarón*. This is the lane which skirts the *Panaítsa* churchyard.

The shopkeepers and craftsmen that may have dwelt in the quarter have moved their premises elsewhere. So the hustle and bustle has shifted to the water front and the main street, while the quiet of the old lanes has a melancholy undertone.

Another melancholy sight is Kokkari's first public water well, just where you turn right when walking from St. Nicholas to the *Platía*. But you will miss it unless you turn left for about five metres, and then take a U-turn. Lo and behold: A tap is inserted in a wall on the left, with an inscription above it that says: "During the Hegemony of *K. I. Fotiádis* / was built and presented this well / from far away bringing the water / 1876."

The original well was most probably a spout with continuously running water, until it was replaced by a tap (which can still be used). Considering that ground water from wells so close to the sea shore would have been a hazardous convenience, and that cisterns were not much better, a well with a good and reliable water supply was certainly a step forward. Perhaps it was the first water pipe directly from the *Mána* Spring.

Villas, Warehouses, and Taverns

Between the parish church and the *Platía*, just opposite the little bakery, a gate is inserted in a stone wall topped by some iron railings. It allows a view into a pretty little garden with a nice little mansion in the background.

This was the villa of *Ioánnis Elissavítis*, the wealthy Kokkarian to whom the completion of the parish church is owed (▷ p. 54). He had developed a wholesale trading firm into the leading enterprise of the village. The ruins of the warehouse are on the north side of the main road, parallel to the *Panaítsa* church.

As a consequence of his commercial success, *Elissavítis* was possibly the most influential person in Kokkari in the first half of the 20th century, excepting of course the *pápas* (parish priest). The family is now extinct, and it can only be hoped that the new owners  will keep the villa in good shape.

Another handsome villa hides behind a hedge some metres to the right of the pharmacy. On the whole, however, Kokkari has less outstanding architecture in store than, for example, some villages in the vicinity of *Karlóvassi*. On the contrary, a walk through the lanes will disclose rather an unpretentious range of dwellings.

Some smaller warehouses in the typical raw quarry stone masonry can be found on the *Kámbos* side of the Beach Street. The peculiar design may have provided moderate humidity and moderate temperatures inside to keep the goods from deterioration. Occasionally a plaque above the door or on the wall displays the name or emblem of the trading enterprise, denoting for instance a wine or olive collection point.

These buildings may be quite old, for example the one opposite the Profile Beach Bar. The badly weathered inscription apparently reads: Κυρ. Χ. Ιερος, 1859, „Lord Christ, the Holy". Underneath the author proposes to make out a plant in a pot (or chalice?) between two fish.

On the main street, opposite the sanctuary of St. Nicholas, Η Μπίρα (*I Bíra*, "The Beer") stands out as Kokkari's most prestigious tavern. It was founded as a *mezedopolíon* (tentative translation: "snack and fruit bar") and commands a strategic location: When opened by *Artémis Mylonás* in 1925, the firm belief that the work at the new parish church would be resumed one day must have inspired the innkeeper. The construction trade is known as a thirsty business all over the world, and so the first Kokkari pub to sell beer must have been an overwhelming success as soon as the works restarted in 1933.

Today's *Bíra* enjoys a reputation as a very traditional tavern, with its surprisingly spacious though rather dark saloon, and with its snug little beer garden under the crooked plane – which is also very popular with the cats of the neighbourhood as a climbing opportunity.

While you are there, cast a look at the stately two-storeyed building across the street, next to the parish church. –

"Manos Bar" at the *Platía* was founded at about the same time as the *Bíra*, but has developed a different character.

The Arch and the Watermills

Everybody who first sets out on the hiking trail up to *Vourliótes* wonders at the arch (▷ rear cover; map ▷ p. 144) not far from the greenhouses. It is part of an aqueduct that was fed by water from the *Mána* spring and provided the headwater for at least two mills. About nine tenths of this water duct can still be traced, albeit as a dry, overgrown or earth-filled trough. It was abandoned some decades ago, probably in the 1960s when electricity became available to replace water power.

The main stretch of the duct is believed to have been laid out 300 years ago as a simple earthen canal. The concrete trough of our days was only built in 1957, according to *Giakoúmis Amyrsónis.*

This trough has a clearance of 35-40 centimetres across and 25-30 high. It received its water from the *Mána* brook, the only stream in Kokkari that offers a water flow of some significance throughout the year. The intake can be reached from the ford that crosses the brook towards the chapel of St. *Pandeleímonas* (▷ p. 107), following the brook's right bank downstream for about 100 metres. A long concrete supporting wall suggests that there may have been a pond, dammed up by a weir. Such a pond would not only have guaranteed a steady flow of the water in the duct, but would also have added to the so-called head (i.e. level difference), which was a vital technical requirement for the mills.

In the immediate vicinity of the intake point, two ruins can be found on the right bank– obviously no former dwellings, but mills or workshops. They cannot have been powered by the aqueduct in question; perhaps they relied on mill wheels immediately below them at the weir. The roofs were destroyed long ago, one of them by the fall of the fantastic olive tree trunk that can still be seen inside. –

From this starting point the aqueduct first followed the right bank of the brook. Then it turned to the right, traversing a temporarily dry rivulet by a tiny bridge, and subsequently swerved left in a wide curvature to span another rivulet by a trough about 3 metres long and 2 metres above water level. Further down it skirted the hill, below the chapel of *Ioánnis Pródromos*, and reached the top of the arch mentioned above, ready to drive the mill located at the downhill side.

In 2013 the mill ruin was being covered with a new roof. This offered an opportunity for a short look into the interior.

What had seemed just some heap of scrap from outside turned out to be the remnants of a so-called Greek Mill, a design which has been used for more than 2200 years and is considered the very oldest type of watermills!

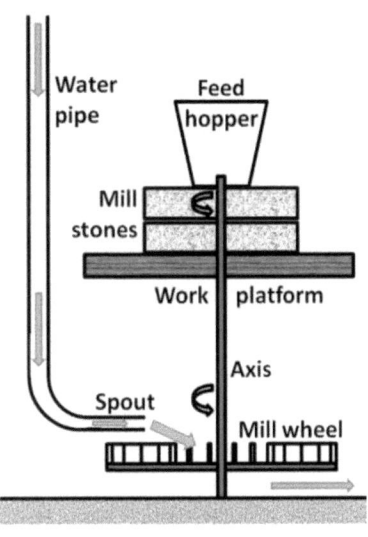

Basically it works as follows: The water must arrive fairly high above the mill building. It falls into a vertical shaft or pipe. At the bottom the pipe has a bend, often with a spout at its end, so that the water is released almost horizontally in a jet. This jet hits an endless row of paddles mounted on a horizontal wheel. The vertical axis of the wheel is extended to the work platform above, where it propels the upper millstone.

In contrast to the traditional watermills of Western Europe with their vertical mill wheel and horizontal axis, this design needs no bevel gear. But its efficiency is considerably lower in comparison. According to *G. Amyrsónis*, one of whose ancestors had founded the mill in 1892, it turned out that in this particular case the head was not really sufficient, so that the mill was soon nicknamed *Koutsómylos*, "Limp Mill".

The aqueduct did not end here. When the mill was in operation, the water splashed down from the horizontal mill wheel and ran outside into a lower trough which continued the aqueduct. Otherwise the water flow could be diverted round the building's walls into the same trough. So nothing was lost, and the water could be used again.

The duct continued on the downhill side of the cart track. At the saddle  250 metres away there must have been a fork. The left branch headed for the mill tower at the foot of the hill, where Kokkari's Beach Street joins the bypass. These 200 metres of the duct were removed when the road uphill was expanded and asphalted. But the ruin of the tower, a conspicuous landmark (map ▷ p. 144), shows how much head the water had at this point. And they say the Beach Mill, or just short "the Mill", was a commercial success indeed. It is still commemorated by the nearby hotel *Mýlos Beach*.

The advantage of a water mill, as opposed to a windmill, was that the water flow was more reliable throughout the year and could be provided as needed. Of course in summer the *meltémi* winds can be quite strong and constant. But here we are concerned with oil mills, and the olive crop in late autumn required mill power in the winter months. On the other hand it is possible that also grain or the like was ground in the course of the year. –

The other branch of the aqueduct followed the contour lines of the hills further east. The best-preserved section is found when ascending the lane leading south from the bypass at about 250 metres from the Beach Mill. In the immediate vicinity of the last house, halfway up to the ridge, the trough is clearly visible on both sides of the lane. The final trace of the duct seems to be on the foothill above some workshop ruins another 250 metres along the bypass.

According to *G. Amyrsónis*, this branch was never intended to provide water power to more mills, but was used for irrigation. There was in fact hardly a chance to establish sufficient head. And as long as the mill at the beach needed the full water flow, other mills would have been idle. At any rate there must have been some mechanism at the fork to steer the water flow to the right when the lower mill was not in operation.

Footpaths, Donkeys, and Goats

Before the arrival of four-wheeled vehicles, the main means of transportation on Samos were the *gaïdoúri*, the donkey, and the *moulári*, the mule. And the usual traffic network on land consisted of footpaths in either of two characteristic shapes: the *monopáti* and the *kalderími*. Today most of them have been replaced by cart tracks, enabling an easy access to the hills by off-road vehicles and pickups – and, lest it be forgotten, by the fire engines in case of bush fires.

A *monopáti* was a single-file footpath. It would not only be used by pedestrians, but also by donkeys and mules carrying voluminous bags on their wooden pack saddles. So it was necessary to keep an appropriate profile clear of rocks and vegetation on both sides of the track. Most of Kokkari's *monopátia* have now made way for farm roads or forest tracks. But two of those which still exist must be mentioned for the romantic hikes they offer. Incidentally they also demonstrate that any encounter of laden mules may have required very careful manoeuvring!

First, there is the footpath up to the chapel of *Profítis Ilias* and further up to *Giánnides*. Here the underground

is mainly soil, due to the routeing along the scarp to the gully. In former times the trail was probably the main access to *Giánnides*; perhaps it had already been used by the *Mytilinií* settlers around 1600.

Second, the footpath to the *Vourliótes* pass along the slope of the *Mána* valley must be mentioned. Here the underground is sometimes sheer rock, though of a soft consistence, and worn out in centuries by the feet of men and animals. In some places the typical sequence of human steps – left, right, left – can still be recognized.

The open view across the valley is actually a very recent feature of the path. Before the bushfire in the year 2000 the slope was wooded in rather the same way as the stretch beyond the pass at the upper end of the valley.

The question if there were also *kalderímia* around Kokkari needs further research. Such paths were to old Samos what motorways are to our times. The typical *kalderími* was wide enough for two laden mules to pass by each other easily. And it was paved, often with steps to prevent heavy rainfall from washing out the track. As paving material local rock might be used, occasionally even marble.

A quite well-preserved *kalderími* is still extant on the steep section of the *Vourliótes* trail several hundred meters beyond the upper end of the *Mána* valley.

As far as the donkeys and mules are concerned, they were still omnipresent in the photos from the 1940s and 1950s. Nowadays they have practically disappeared. Only in the vicinity of the pass toward *Mytilinií* one or two of these animals can occasionally be seen grazing. They belong to the solitary farm up there. And with a lot of luck one may even come across an animal equipped with the traditional wooden pack saddle.

Goats are a different case. As the history of *Aiogdítes* shows (▷ p. 99), these animals have always been around in the area. Although goat breeding may have become a rare trade, there are still some goat herds roaming in the region. And occasionally a hiker may trust a seeming shortcut, only to find that it is just a goat path leading into nowhere...

But even in such a nowhere the wanderer can hit on a collection of colourful beehives. Against a widespread assumption the bees are not needed to pollinate the olive trees, but produce a delicious honey from wild flowers and herbs.

Onions, Olives, and Orchids

The Samos Yearbook of 1875 proudly quotes the complete annual onion production of the island: more than 25,000 κανταρίων (from *kantári*, literally "hand-scales"; actually a historical weight of 56.5 kilograms). Among the three quality grades, the oblong κοκκάρια were the smallest und cheapest size, sold at 8 γρόσια, "groats", per *kantári*.

What does this mean with regard to the etymology of the name *Kokkari*? The product appellation confirms that the little red onions were generally associated with the village. The root *kokk-* ties up to *kókkino kremmídi,* red onion. Is the form *kokkári* a diminutive or affectionate variation?

Red onions of various sizes, but no kokkária...

The traditional explanation is that these onions were a favourite crop in the Kokkari area and lent their name to the village. But the case is not as simple as it seems. Considering that the name *Kokar*, denoting either a place or a person, was documented as early as 1601, the "onion" hypothesis could also be a popular etymology invented in retrospect; in other words, the name shared by the village and the onions might be derived from the earliest settlers. In an attempt to reconcile the two variants, let us assume that *Kokkári*, "Little Red Onion", was the surname or nickname of the very first settler, a man who brought those modest vegetables to the northern shores of Samos – not only as a cultivator, but also as a gourmet...

What has become of Kokkari's eponymous onions nowadays? Their cultivation was more or less superseded by other crops, especially wine, in the early 20th century. They may occasionally still be grown for home use. At any rate there seems to be no advertising for local or regional sale. At the Kokkari groceries you can

131

of course buy onions, mostly red ones, to be sure. But their size betrays that they have outgrown the oblong "little onions" of yore. –

While the onions have apparently accompanied Kokkari from the beginning, the greenhouses (map ▷ p. 144) in the vicinity of the Limp Mill Arch disclose a very recent branch of agriculture, or rather horticulture. In 1979, Kokkari-born *Giakoúmis Amyrsónis* started the production of orchids in these greenhouses. After studying flower cultivation in Pisa, Italy, he had decided to build up his own firm. In 1986 he transferred its main location to southern Samos, between *Chóra* and *Mýli*. But the Kokkari greenhouses are still in operation, with tens of thousands of plants. *Amyrsónis* deals with only one orchid species, *Cymbidium*, but this species fans out in a rich diversity of forms and colours. The enterprise is said to be the only orchid cultivator in Greece; it mainly supplies the capital, Athens, where it has an outlet.

Back to more traditional branches of agriculture! A peculiar side effect of the recent bushfires was the discovery of how diligently former generations worked the sparse soil of the hills far away from the village. Especially the terraces with their low supporting walls made of undressed stone (hence *pezoúlia*, little walls) are witnesses of their industriousness. Still today they are an effective remedy against erosion.

Olive trees can become several centuries old. Where they are still cultivated today, a bottle or canister hung up in a tree may indicate that the grove has been treated with some sort of pesticide. Other growers, devoted to organic farming, are proud that they use no such chemical substances. In either case, the olives are harvested late in the year, when the tourist season is over.

The vineyards, on the other hand, are harvested in summer, almost at the peak season. This may be the reason why Kokkari's viniculture has severely dwindled.

There are, however, at least two local winemakers who sell their own wine, one of them on Beach Street, opposite the last houses on the beach side, and the other in the lane that can be reached from the small bridge near the sharp turn of the main street into Beach Street. The vintners are not allowed to tag the bottles with labels of their own – but their wine is delicious!

In former times not only wine was produced, but also *soúma*, a pomace brandy, the local version of *tsípouro*. After passing the Limp Mill Arch on the trail to

Vourliótes, a few metres to the left from the point where the path hits the first dry rivulet, three stone rings mark subterranean cavities. When the grapes had been crushed to yield the wine, the remaining mash, the pomace, was put in these cavities for fermentation before the brandy could be distilled. –

An appraisal of Kokkari's agricultural sector today will arrive at the conclusion that many of the old fields and groves are still cultivated, but many others are fallow now or have fallen into oblivion.

Ruins and Rivulets

Only three column stumps are left of the ancient Asklepeios sanctuary (c. 500 BC) at the so-called *Mána* Spring. Its location at the aperture of the steep *Mána* gorge was apparently induced by a waterfall of the brook. Later torrential rains must have rearranged the rocks and boulders from time to time, creating different channels for the water. Local sources say that in 1936 a new waterfall was created in this way, but in 2001 the brook disappeared into the almost invisible outlet of today. –

When Arab raids began to threaten the Aegean Sea in the course of the 7th century AD, the fortress called *Cástro Louloudás* offered a safe refuge. The archaeological evidence is summarized by *K. Tsákos* as follows: "Stepped streets cut in the rock led to houses that stood on rock-cut terraces, exploiting the flat roofs of the underlying houses towards which these extended. The last fortification evidently dates from Middle Byzantine times but the cuttings in the rock for the foundations of structures and the sherds of ancient vases point to occupation of the naturally fortified crag since antiquity." There was even a simple church. *Louloúdas*, as *Tsákos* asserts, is derived from *láas*, "stone", "rock" (not from *louloúdi*, "flower", "blossom").

The access to the precipitous peak includes a dangerous passage which persons suffering from vertigo should not attempt. At any rate the sight of the few remnants from which the conclusions quoted above are drawn may be a disappointment. –

The following ruins take us to the Modern Period.

Solitary masonry, scattered over the remote parts of the old neighbourhoods, recalls the time when the farmers lived in the hills during the summer months, in order to be closer to their fields and groves.

In contrast to these secluded cabins, the little settlement next to the *Profítis Ilías* chapel in lower *Giánnides* must have been used by people who preferred social contact

– and who used to bake their own bread, as the oven witnesses.

The ruins in *Vígles* near the *Agios Dimítrios* chapel may even have been a permanent settlement. The large blocks of stone are a building material seldom found elsewhere in the area. And in comparison to the *Profítis Ilías* cottages they were less conspicuous from the sea.

In contrast to the sparse hills, the marsh land of the *Kámbos* provided a fertile soil; here the problem was not erosion, but poor drainage. An attentive observation of the terrain on both sides of the Beach Street reveals that the level of the *Kámbos* side is considerably lower than the beach front. In times of strong rainfall the marsh may soak the humidity until parts of it are flooded (like every now and then the car parks!). So the pump work near the bypass, not far from the western head of the sports ground, is a very useful installation. It discharges the water into the brook that runs through the village centre and into the bay. Of course there is not much water around to be pumped during the summer drought, so this brook may seasonally present a sorry sight. As a matter of fact it is simply called *Réma*. The word means a rivulet that usually falls dry in summer.

After torrential winter rains, the brooks from the hills constitute a different and often greater danger. The most precarious watercourse in this respect may be the brook from *Giánnides*. As it emerges from its ravine below *Profítis Ilías*, it is channelled into the cart track towards the village. In case of a flood the water is kept inside a hollow way for several hundred metres. But when the water flow has passed under the bypass bridge, its level is a metre or more above the adjacent fields. So a dam had to be built with a wide channel on top to prevent the flooding of the plain. Under every-day conditions it just serves as a street, facilitating the access to the houses in the *Kámbos* from the bypass. In case of a torrent this area may escape the flood, but the continuation of the canalised road puts the riparians towards the Beach Street in jeopardy before the flow eventually passes into the sea.

Military Memories

During the wars between Greece and Turkey from 1912 to 1923, Samos was not involved as a combat area. But even so the conflict had its local repercussions: The memorial stele next to St. Nicholas, opposite *I Bíra*, shows a list of 24 Kokkarians who lost their lives as soldiers in those wars – one officer, two non-commissioned officers, and 21 privates.

There is no similar local memorial to the victims of the Second World War or to those of the Italian and German occupation, let alone the subsequent civil war. There are, however, some other traces of military significance.

The narrow lane from the *Limáni* roundabout along the west face of the peninsula ends after 25 metres at some large rocks – or so it seems. Some of the rocks are made of concrete, and on close inspection the ruins of a pillbox can be recognized. How long has it been here? The layout resembles quite closely a German "Ringstand" model, built by the thousands during the Second World War. This brings us to the year in which Samos was occupied by the German "Wehrmacht" (Nov. 1943 to 4 Oct. 1944). The purpose, in this case, would have been to repel any Allied landing attempts. Whether the simpler ruin at the isthmus to the Cavos peninsula goes back to the same time is not quite clear.

On the hill above the Beach Mill ruin a strange trove is hidden which seemed to be unknown even to many native Kokkarians in 2013. The hill can be ascended from the back by a rather inconspicuous footpath. At the top a shed of corrugated iron shelters a veritable tank with a Greek Army emblem.

A "panzer" left here by the Germans when they had to evacuate Samos precipitously in 1944? Very unlikely, because there would have been no need to hide it in a shed. It would rather have been displayed publicly as a victory memorial.

Without anticipating an expert's identification, the tank could be a Cold War model, such as an American M 48 "Patton". The rusty vehicle still boasts a turret and a muzzle, but it seems that most of the valuable innards, as it were, have gone. The only imaginable reason why it should have been brought up here is the protection of Kokkari's Long Beach against invasions. The question is: when? Maybe during the tense relations to Turkey during the 1970s? Especially at the time of the Cyprus Crisis in 1974? –

As far as the 21st century is concerned, an attentive observer will soon recognise some of the present-day military installations on Samos, and also within the limits of Kokkari. The impression is that the island is more strongly fortified than ever against any invaders, whoever they may be...

Appendix

Sources and Supporters

"No man is an island", said John Donne in the 17th century. And the author can only assent: He has profited indeed from information of all kind, supplied with good grace, or unwittingly, by knowledgeable people. So here is an emphatic thank you to all those who have contributed – not only to those whose names are mentioned below, but to quite a few others who may not even be aware that their information has been incorporated in this booklet.

As far as the history of Samos is concerned, the pictorial guide written by *K. Tsakos* has provided a useful general orientation: Konstantinos Tsakos, *Samos. A guide to the history and archaeology*. Athens: Hesperos Editions, 2003.

It was complemented by an internet publication of some local historians, Christos Landros and his co-authors: http://www2.egeonet.gr/aigaio

And there was a last-minute discovery: Kristina Holzhausen, *Samos: 1821-1920*. Saarbrücken: VDM Verlag Dr. Müller, 2011.

For many other aspects, however, and especially for the 20th century, some patient research by the author proved necessary, including the verification or refutation of details reported in various Samos maps and tourist guides.

As far as Kokkari's churches and chapels are concerned, the most important local source was "*Exoklísia*", a scholastic project. It was realized some years ago by 6 Kokkarian students aged about 12 to 14: *G. Volakákis, P. Diakogiánni, M. Zavoudákis, E. Zíou, K. Kámfouras* and *D. Filippéou*. Their main oral history source, apart from the parish priest, was *G. Amyrsónis*, who is said to know more about Kokkari than anybody else. The mentor of the 6 students, teacher *G. Tsardoúlias*, helped them to collect their research in a Powerpoint file in December 2012. In May 2014 the Kokkari parish priest, *Pápa Giórgos*, kindly provided the author with a copy of the file on CD. *G. Moutafis*, a professor emeritus of history, was a great help in translating the Greek texts.

The hagiographic passages, i.e. the lives of the saints, have been derived from various sources, especially from specialised Greek-Orthodox web sites such as www.orthodoxwiki.org and www.orthpedia.de. This internet research was backed up by a general knowledge accumulated by the author in a lifelong experience as a history teacher with some interest in ecclesiastical history.

For the secular section, local information was contributed not only by native Kokkarians, notably *G. Amyrsónis* and Professor *V. Galánis-Moutáfis*, but also by new residents from the Greek mainland or from abroad, and even by tourists of many years of Samos experience, in particular *R. Brockmeyer*.

Last but not least, a circumspect use of Wikipedia was unavoidable – mainly the English and German sites, occasionally the Greek and French ones.

The illustrations, as far as they concern Kokkari directly (photos, sketches, maps) have been generated by the author himself. All other material of this sort has been checked as public domain.

Postscript

A very recent browsing visit to the internet site of the German National Military Archive has yielded three remarkable results: 1. The German invasion of Samos, "Operation Damokles", was undertaken by "Kampf-gruppe Müller", part of the 22nd Infantry Division. (General Friedrich-Wilhelm Müller, called the "Butcher of Greece" after massacres on Crete and Kos, was executed in Athens in 1947.) – 2. Documents on the operation are available in the archive. – 3. There may also be documents on the occupation of Samos, of course from the German perspective.

But this sounds like a project that must be postponed for the time being.

Map: Village Centre

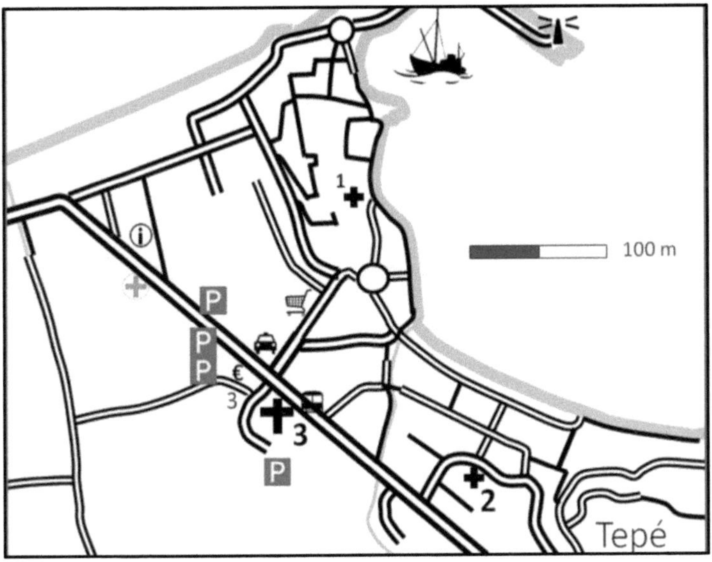

Map: Neighbourhoods West

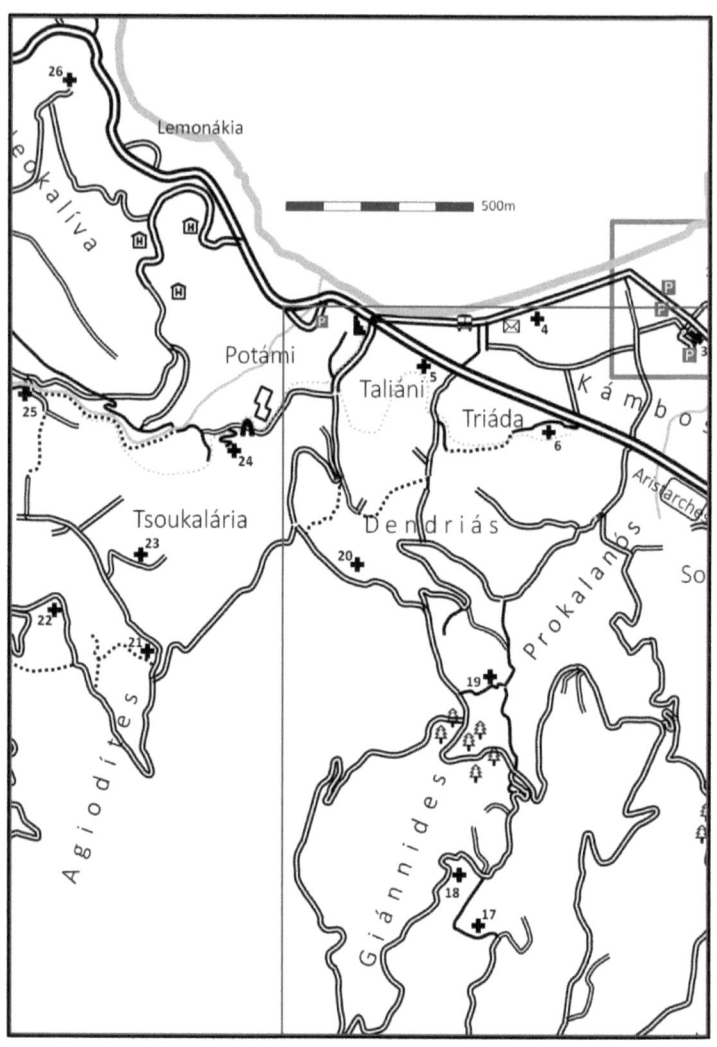

Map: Neighbourhoods South

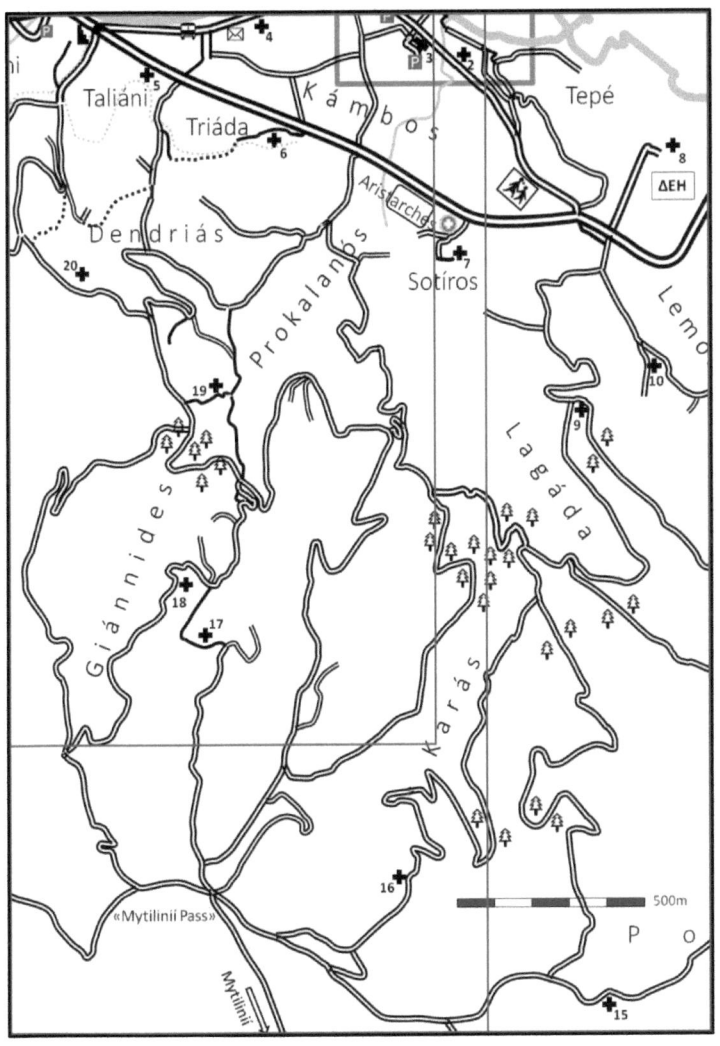

Map: Neighbourhoods East

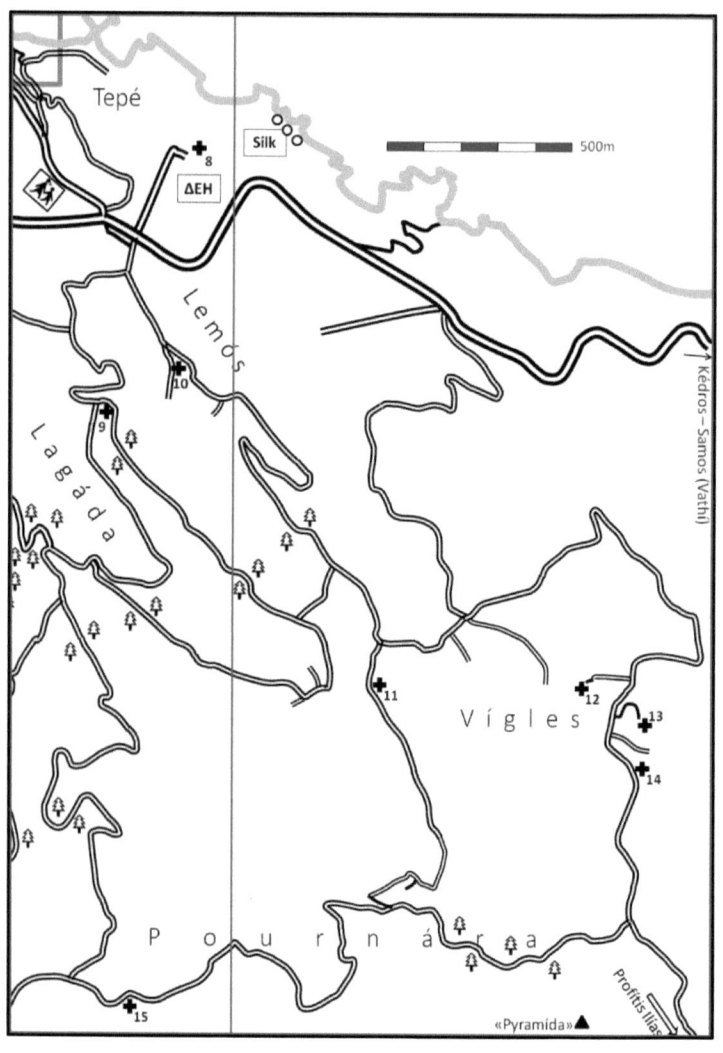

Tepé

Silk

ΔEH

8

Lemós

Lagáda

10

9

Kédros – Samos (Vathi)

500m

11

Vígles

12

13

14

Pournária

15

Profitis Ilías

«Pyramída» ▲